Modern Arab American Fiction

Arab American Writing

OTHER TITLES IN ARAB AMERICAN WRITING

Bread Alone
KIM JENSEN

Does the Land Remember Me? A Memoir of Palestine
AZIZ SHIHAB

Letters from Cairo
PAULINE KALDAS

Loom: A Novel
THÉRÈSE SOUKAR CHEHADE

Love Is Like Water and Other Stories
SAMIA SERAGELDIN

The Man Who Guarded the Bomb: Stories
GREGORY ORFALEA

The New Belly Dancer of the Galaxy: A Novel
FRANCES KHIRALLAH NOBLE

Remember Me to Lebanon: Stories of Lebanese Women in America
EVELYN SHAKIR

Swimming Toward the Light: A Novel
ANGELA TEHAAN LEONE

Through and Through: Toledo Stories, 2d ed.
JOSEPH GEHA

MODERN
ARAB AMERICAN
FICTION

A Reader's Guide

STEVEN
SALAITA

SYRACUSE UNIVERSITY PRESS

Mohamad El-Hindi Books on Arab Culture and Islamic Civilization are published with the assistance of a grant from the M.E.H. Foundation.

∞ The paper used in this publication meets the minimum requirements of the American National Standard for Information Sciences—Permanence of Paper for Printed Library Materials, ANSI Z39.48-1992.

For a listing of books published and distributed by Syracuse University Press, visit our Web site at SyracuseUniversityPress.syr.edu.

ISBN: 978-0-8156-3277-1 (cloth)
ISBN: 978-0-8156-3253-5 (paper)

Library of Congress Cataloging-in-Publication Data

Salaita, Steven, 1975–
Modern Arab American fiction : a reader's guide / Steven Salaita. — 1st ed.
p. cm. — (Arab American writing)
Includes bibliographical references and index.
ISBN 978-0-8156-3277-1 (cloth : alk. paper) — ISBN 978-0-8156-3253-5 (pbk. : alk. paper)
1. American fiction—Arab American authors—History and criticism.   2. American fiction—
20th century—History and criticism.   3. Arab Americans in literature.
4. Arabs in literature.   I. Title.
PS153.A73S33 2011
813'.54098927—dc22   2010052845

Manufactured in the United States of America

Steven Salaita is an associate professor of English at Virginia Tech. His other books include *Anti-Arab Racism in the USA: Where It Comes from and What It Means for Politics Today; Arab American Literary Fictions, Culture, and Politics;* and *The Holy Land in Transit* (Syracuse University Press, 2006).

Contents

Modern Arab American Fiction

1

Introduction

IN ADDITION TO BEING a user-friendly analysis of modern Arab American fiction, this book is something of a corrective for bad luck. This unusual mission is a selfish one. I do not intend for the book to correct your bad luck. I am not quite so arrogant, though I would be happy if it manages to improve your fortunes somehow. The book instead endeavors to correct my own bad luck. If what I speak of is not technically bad luck, then it is certainly a case of bad timing.

Because being oblique is not one of my goals, I should explain what I mean. A few years ago I was fully ensconced in my newfound interest in Arab American studies. I had developed a particular interest in Arab American fiction, befitting my scholarly training in modern American literature. Arab American studies was then—as, in many ways, now—an emerging subject (even now, we cannot properly call it a field). I encountered wonderful scholarship on various aspects of Arab America, employing assorted disciplinary methodologies, but I did not feel that I found enough. One glaring omission was book-length literary criticism focused specifically on the Arab American tradition. This omission was especially noteworthy given the many books of literary criticism of countless varieties in the current marketplace.

I decided that I would play a role in filling this gap. I made this decision in 2003 and started collecting research shortly thereafter, reading everything I could get my hands on. I spent the entire summer and autumn of 2005 writing the manuscript that eventually was published as *Arab American Literary Fictions, Cultures, and Politics* in January 2007. It ended up being the first book-length study of Arab American literature. An absence in the marketplace had been amended. The gap, however, remains, but I do not imagine that it will be around much longer.

This is where my bad luck comes into play. When *Arab American Literary Fictions, Cultures, and Politics* was in production, I started noticing an upsurge of Arab American novels. These books, of course, were not available as I was composing and editing my manuscript, and they were appearing faster than I could buy and read them. This upsurge was fantastic for the literary and intellectual marketplace in which my book participated, but it was something of an encumbrance for the book itself. I counted around seven or eight Arab American novels published between the time that I submitted my manuscript to the publisher and the moment that the book appeared in print. By the time my book was published, then, it was immediately outdated. That was the best piece of bad luck I have ever experienced.

I consider this bad luck to be a good thing because I am thrilled that Arab American literature is undergoing something of a qualitative and quantitative maturation (I shudder at the word *renaissance*). I also feel good about this bad luck because I now have an excuse to write another book of Arab American literary criticism. I am aware that by the time what I am now writing becomes an actual book, it too will be outdated. Indeed, the plan I have devised for it will probably change frequently based on developments in publishing and rumors of work in progress. This generation of Arab American novelists is keeping me busy. If they were not, I would have no reason to write, and they would have no ability to claim participation in a literary community. The sort of dynamism now apparent in the Arab American literary tradition is indicative of the healthfulness necessary to assert a categorical distinctiveness. Arab American drama seems to be everywhere these days, produced and performed with wit and ingenuity. Poetry is probably the most established genre in the Arab American literary tradition; it too appears to be flourishing, constantly promising to break new ground and rarely defaulting. But fiction, especially the novel, has emerged in the past decade as a formidable art form in the Arab American community. Ten years ago, when I first became interested in Arab American writing, I could read the entire novelistic canon in less than a month (something I actually did). Now a backlog of novels crowds my "to read" bookshelf. So I begin this project, unlike the previous one, with the material distinctly outpacing my ambition.

Beyond a corrective for bad luck, this book is intended to be both a primer and a critical analysis. I do not necessarily see a contradiction between the terms *primer* and *critical analysis,* although I confess that they are not meant to go together. Primers usually are very basic introductions to or explications of (usually complex) subjects. Critical analyses usually transform the basic into something complex (which is not always a good thing). My goal is to combine the mandate of critical analysis with the accessibility of the primer in order to provide readers with an overview of the modern Arab American novel that is neither simplistic nor esoteric. *Modern Arab American Fiction* endeavors to be thorough, serious, and appropriate for a variety of readers. I hope that students and lay readers interested in Arab American writing will find it a useful source of contextual information and that professional literary critics whose livelihoods depend on their analyses of Arab American writing will find it of critical value. Perhaps these dual goals are unduly ambitious. I do believe, though, that a well-written book can transcend archetypal (or presupposed) reading proclivities. If this were not the case, then it would be impossible for me, somebody whose livelihood is certainly dependent on performing literary criticism, to enjoy poetry, diplomatic histories, gossip magazines, political biographies, and comic books simultaneously. Permit me, then, to suggest immodestly that whatever the level of your critical training or interest in Arab American fiction, this book will be of interest to you.

An Overview of Modern Arab American Fiction

Before we get to the literary criticism, let us take a look at some contextual issues. You might have noticed that I have been using phrases such as "Arab American novels," "Arab American literary criticism," and "Arab American studies." These phrases do not necessarily have obvious meanings, so I would like to focus on them for a moment. Although I believe it is problematic to spend lots of time working out the meanings of imprecise terms and phrases at the expense of literary criticism, I also think it is important to acknowledge that the categories we often take for granted are not usually as trenchant as we may first imagine them to be. By thinking about their complexity, we can learn much about how literature functions in historical, cultural, and political frameworks.

Within the spectrum of American literary traditions, Arab American literature is relatively new. Writing produced by Americans of Arab origin is a product mainly of the twentieth century and started to develop exponentially only in the past thirty years. As a category that we use to organize college classes, professional organizations, and bookshelves, "Arab American literature" is remarkably new. Although the phrase has been used here and there ever since Arabs began writing in the United States, as an institutional category "Arab

American literature" is still a teenager. It has been solidified within the past two decades. These days you can find the phrase all over college syllabi, book jackets, and conference panels as well as in the pages of scholarly journals and major newspapers such as the *New York Times*. Syracuse University Press even has an entire series devoted to Arab American writing, and other university and corporate presses have allocated resources to the publication of Arab American work. "Arab American literature," in other words, is legitimizing itself by participating in the scholarly and popular institutions that lend credence to classifications that are inherently abstract.

So what is Arab American literature? I will be honest and confess that, despite my devotion to Arab American literature, I do not really know how to answer this question in a straightforward way. Different people answer (and ask) it in different ways. I have had many a debate, some of them intense, around this seemingly simple question. On principle, a part of me does not like to offer an answer: in answering the question, we risk reducing literature, an unfettered art form, into something tethered to its producers' perceived cultural authenticity. Nevertheless, if we are to speak of an "Arab American literature," then it is necessary to put forward a working definition, even if we acknowledge that it will be inadequate. (Even if we do not state a working definition, we would be adhering to one implicitly.)

Here is what I have in mind when using the phrase "Arab American literature" in this book (a working definition that influenced which novels I chose to include in my analysis): Arab American literature consists of creative work produced by American authors of Arab origin and that participates, in a conscious way or through its critical reception, in a category that has come to be known as "Arab American literature." Unless, of course, it does not actually participate in the category. Unless, furthermore, the writer is a Canadian citizen. Unless the work participates very strongly in the category of "Arab American literature" but has an author of non-Arab Middle Eastern ethnicity. And unless . . . OK, OK, I'll stop. You get the point. These exceptions to the definition I posted are intended not merely as sarcasm, but as illustrations of the fact that when you enter into a study of Arab American literature, you find something diverse and heterogeneous. In thinking about the works that compose Arab American literature, I tend to emphasize the writer's ethnic origin in addition to thematic content, although no literary category has hard and fast criteria; all categories are riddled with exceptions and a lack of airtight logic. The fact is that nobody will ever put together an analysis of an ethnic literary tradition that makes complete sense in terms of its choices of inclusion and exclusion. In literary criticism, we may seek sound logic, but the actual world of literature is too complex to figure out using mechanical organizational systems. This complexity is a wonderful thing.

It stands to reason, then, that Arab American literary criticism is not as concrete as black words on white paper. The same problems of categorization that exist around Arab American literature also apply to Arab American literary criticism. The only distinction of interest is the fact that Arab American literature is better developed than its critical partner. There is no large volume of work in the Arab American critical tradition, but practitioners of Arab American literary criticism are now being hired in universities and drawing interest from scholarly presses. A small but devoted group of young scholars is currently producing study after study highlighting numerous dimensions of Arab life in the United States. Taken together, these studies, whether social, political, or cultural, are helping to develop an Arab American critical apparatus in which the analysis of literature contributes and participates. The inclusion of Arab American literature in intellectual discussions and in the university study of American culture now appears to be lasting. Arab American literary criticism focuses on the dimensions of Arab American cultural and political life that have something to do with the production and reception of literature.

The multidisciplinary explorations of Arab life in the United States can be said to compose an Arab American studies. Do actual Arab American studies departments and programs exist, as Native American studies and Asian American studies do? At this point, no. (See how new all of this stuff really is?) This absence does not mean that Arab American studies is merely an invention, however. The University of Michigan–Ann Arbor has a small but remarkably productive program in Arab American studies housed in its prestigious Program in American Culture. Because of this program and the presence of faculty in other departments who specialize in Arab America, the university is a center of Arab American scholarship. Its neighbor, the University of Michigan–Dearborn, houses the Center for Arab American Studies, which offers both undergraduate and graduate degrees. Other universities have hired faculty to help install Arab American studies in their curricula. Although one still cannot attain a Ph.D. in a field called Arab American studies, one can focus on Arab American studies in earning a Ph.D. A common and productive way to do that is through the study of Arab American literature.

Arab American studies is concerned with numerous issues of interest to Arab American writers and critics: American foreign policy in the Arab and Muslim worlds; the representation of Arabs in popular culture; the movements and trajectories of diasporic Arab communities; and a plethora of sociocultural issues tied into gender, race, and identity. This nascent area study is attracting the attention and participation of scholars from around the world. Many a conference panel has discussed where an Arab American studies best fits into the spectrum of academic disciplines. In particular, people have debated whether Arab American studies should push for better representation within the field of Middle East studies or is better suited for American or ethnic studies paradigms. This question seems a bit frivolous, but the way people address it speaks to what they imagine the possibilities and limitations of an Arab American studies to be. I, for instance, argue that Arab American studies is best developed within the framework of various American landscapes and should therefore avoid becoming a mere subset or branch of Middle East studies. By making this argument, I am stating an ethical position that Arab Americans are fundamentally of the United States. I am also putting forward a strategy for growth. Most important, I am suggesting possibilities for productive scholarly interchange. This suggestion is an important feature of Arab American scholarship: most of its practitioners are interested in both scholarly and political dialogue with other ethnic American communities. As you shall see, the same is certainly true of Arab American fiction writers.

A Breakdown of Modern Arab American Fiction

One thing that literary critics like to do that drives some authors mad is to parcel literature into different categories. As a critic, I would like to defend my hyper-logical comrades by pointing out that it is nearly impossible to create college classes, reading lists, or literary communities without relegating books to different classes (the basis of categorization). Critics are not the only guilty parties, though. Publishers and booksellers also invent and sustain literary categories that are fundamentally illogical (which, I should point out, is not yet illegal). Think about it: How would you know where to find a book on, say, Indian boarding schools if your local Barnes & Noble did not have a section called "Native American studies"? The publishers are often the ones who instruct the bookstores where to shelve different titles. Pick up any of your books and look at the upper-right corner of the back cover. Do you see a classification? Maybe it says "history" or "political science." It might provide a cluster of options: "sociology/Asian American studies" or "Middle East studies/literary criticism," for example. You have just witnessed the use of literary categories. If you are a student, you witness it every time you register for English classes as well.

What does all of this have to do with modern Arab American fiction? A great deal, actually. The point I am trying to make is that Arab American literature is highly varied even if individual works get lumped into the same category. Encountering a novel or a book of poems classified as "Arab American" does not mean that it will look a particular way or cover a predetermined set of themes. "Arab American literature" refers merely to a body of work that shares an affinity according to authors, publishers, readers, booksellers, literature teachers, or all of them in an unspoken concordance. It is a descriptive category, not a prescriptive one. No stable features exist consistently in the work that is described as "Arab American." Why in the world, then, do we still uphold the category? First, because even if we cannot find a set of stable features in Arab American work, we can detect some motifs and dynamics that justify the existence of the category. More important, like all such groupings, "Arab American literature" is a *political* category, not a cultural or historical given. Various people have put it together, and I designate it "political" because it is not a blueprint of actual literature; it is mainly a way for this literature to find a niche and an audience and a way for critics to pursue coherent forms of investigation of that literature. However, it is important to remember that the category "Arab American literature," whatever its inconsistencies, is very real. It is a legitimate label with a growing presence in publishers' catalogs and educational curricula.

What motifs and dynamics can you expect to find when you open an "Arab American novel"? You will encounter numerous styles and aesthetics, many of which can be found in other American literary traditions. You will also encounter some themes recurrent in those traditions: immigration, assimilation, racism, marginalization, return to origin, and so forth. Some themes appear to be specific to Arab American fiction, though, based on many of its authors' common experiences: the Israel-Palestine conflict; the Lebanese Civil War of 1975–90; the representation and practice of Islam in the United States; anti-Arab racism and Islamophobia; the politics and histories of the Arab world; social issues such as gender and national identity in Arab cultures; and the various identities that come with being Arab American. I have organized this book around these thematic archetypes rather than developing it chronologically. There are many other ways, of course, to organize a study of Arab American fiction, but I have found it most useful to explore modern Arab American novels and short stories based on theme instead of on chronology, national origin, or any other possible way of organizing a book of literary criticism.

I find a thematic organization most useful because it asks us to emphasize the content of the work rather than the logistics of its authorship or date of publication. The chapters in this book situate authors around a cluster of motifs. I hope that this structure allows you to better compare and contrast various authors and to emphasize not just the authors' backgrounds, but also the content and quality of their work. As you read more and more of Arab American fiction, you will find that its subject matter is wide ranging and diverse. This book is intended to highlight that diversity rather than to restrict Arab American fiction to something prescriptive—that is to say, something predetermined by the critic's preferences. Reading is most fun and productive when the reader can create his or her own meaning in response to or in conjunction with an artistic presentation.

I fortunately cannot provide you with a tidy definition of what modern Arab American fiction is. It would be nice to be able to do so—something such as, "Modern Arab American fiction is X." Then we would have the clarity so many of us desire. Why is it fortunate, then, that I cannot proffer such a tidy definition? Because if it were possible to give a tidy definition of this literary tradition, then the tradition would not be worth reading. Arab American novels represent everything that good literature has been and is supposed to be. The main quality all good literature shares is a complexity that makes it difficult to pigeonhole. I hope that after reading some of these heterogeneous novels, you will be able to decide for yourself what best describes modern Arab American fiction.

Reality versus Fiction?

All ethnic literatures arise from communities that imagine themselves to be distinct in some way. If we are to come to an understanding of an Arab American literature, it would be a good idea to examine the community from which it arises.

Let me begin by excluding from the category of "Arab American" some communities that often are erroneously included in it. I make this distinction because lumping discrete communities together is more than merely inaccurate; it is unfair to those communities because it subsumes their culture and history into others that are not theirs. Iranians, Afghans, Turks, and Pakistanis are not Arab. Although these groups are predominantly Muslim, a commonality they share with Arabs, each of them is culturally and linguistically distinct, with its own artistic traditions. Even within the geographical Arab world, there are non-Arab ethnic communities: Berbers, Kurds, Armenians, Chaldeans, Assyrians, Circassians. I have included under the rubric of "Arab American literature" authors from these minority communities insofar as they participate in and identify with the category. These minority communities maintain their own ethnic and historical uniqueness, but they speak Arabic and are located inside Arab nations. If individuals among those communities in the United States choose to participate in Arab American spaces, then I find it reasonable to honor that choice.

Accurate demographics on the Arab American community are difficult to find. However, various estimates indicate that there are approximately three to four million Arab Americans. The biggest national demographic is Lebanese Americans, followed by Syrian, Egyptian, and Palestinian Americans. For many years, pollsters have claimed that 75 percent of Arab Americans are Christian, but some scholars, myself included, have recently modified the number to put it at a range of 40 to 60 percent. At this point, it is safe to assume that roughly half of Arab Americans are Christian, although in the coming years the percentage of Muslim Arab Americans will surely increase. Not all Arab Americans are Muslim and Christian, though; the community includes Druze, Bahai, and Jews, although in small numbers. Muslims include both Sunni and Shia, and the Christians are mainly Catholic and Orthodox, but in total multidenominational.

Arab Americans live all over the United States, although the majority can be found in urban and metropolitan areas. Los Angeles County in California has the largest population of Arab Americans; Wayne County in Michigan has the highest concentration. Indeed, Dearborn, a city adjacent to Detroit, is considered the cultural and political heart of the Arab American community. Members of the Arab American community do not adhere to a particular set of politics; their politics are all over the map and often in conflict. Nor do Arab Americans fit neatly into any social or economic class. This sort of heterogeneity is reflected in the range of experiences and viewpoints that can be found in modern Arab American fiction.

During the first half of the twentieth century, immigrants to the United States from the Arab world consisted mainly of Christians, the majority from Syria and Lebanon. As the United States relaxed its immigration quotas, however, these largely Christian Arab immigrants were joined by Muslim Arabs from North Africa and West Asia. Now the Arab American community is a polyglot comprising both fifth-generation Americans and newly arrived immigrants. The community has changed dramatically from its early immigrant days a century ago and now plays a vital role in the politics, cultures, and economics of the United States.

Despite this widespread presence in American life, Arab Americans are one of the least understood ethnic groups in the United States. Many Americans know little about Arabs and Arab Americans beyond those they see in news broadcasts and popular media, who are represented almost exclusively as idiotic and violent. Thus, the characters you will encounter in modern Arab American fiction will look quite different from the ones you may expect to see. This is not to say that all of these characters are good people. Some of them are vile and violent; others are idiotic. Yet others are kind and loving and heartwarmingly generous. In other words, the characters you will encounter reflect to some degree the complexity of the people who populate Arab America and the world in general. One function (or result) of good literature is to usher readers beyond two-dimensional views of the world and its inhabitants. Engaging Arab American literature is one way to come into a relationship with Middle Eastern ways of being that are more sophisticated than pop culture entanglements. But I would encourage you not to read literature merely to learn culture or to unlearn stereotypes. If these things happen as you read literature, then you should feel happy, but they should not be your primary reason for reading a novel.

Literature is ultimately a form of art. Good art can do many things simultaneously, and its consumers do themselves a delightful favor when they attempt to access as many of its affections as they can. This book cannot perform that task for you, but it can help you develop a critical framework for understanding modern Arab American fiction. Just make sure to keep that framework updated.

2

Uses of the Lebanese Civil War in Arab American Fiction

Etel Adnan, Rawi Hage, Patricia Sarrafian Ward

AT ITS MOST BASIC LEVEL, the Lebanese Civil War pitted Christians against Muslims. (Lebanon has the highest percentage of Christians in the Arab world, followed by Egypt, Syria, Palestine, Jordan, and Iraq. Arab Christians have been a part of the Arab world for more than two thousand years.) The war specifically involved Sunni Muslims and Maronite Christians. Many of the Sunni Muslim combatants were Palestinians, who compose a large underclass in Lebanon, having been expelled from Palestine in 1948 and residing mainly in a series of refugee camps. By the mid-1970s, the Palestinians had formed a powerful, militarized bloc that existed outside the authority of the Lebanese state. This bloc was threatening to the Maronite Christians and cumbersome to a delicate power-sharing arrangement among Lebanon's seventeen cultural and religious communities.

Lebanon is a former French colony, its borders carved delicately in Paris in the 1920s to produce a slight Christian majority, one that would presumably be friendly to France and to Western interests more generally. In subsequent decades, however, heavy Christian emigration and higher Muslim birthrates prevented Christians from remaining Lebanon's largest religious group. Shiite Muslims, once Lebanon's third-largest group, soon became its largest. Sunni Muslims remained second. The constitution set up in the 1920s distributed power based on demographics that soon became arcane. In Lebanon, the president must be a Maronite Christian (Orthodox and Protestant Christians are excluded), the prime minister a Sunni Muslim, and the speaker of Parliament a Shiite Muslim. Governing a country and making laws based on demography is always a rickety venture, so it probably surprised few people outside of Paris that Lebanon faced civil conflict in 1958 (eventually involving American marines) and again in 1973. What is usually called the "Lebanese Civil War" is the fighting that occurred from 1975 to 1990, although these dates are not accepted universally among scholars and commentators.

When a large Palestinian refugee population, mostly Sunni Muslim, entered into Lebanon in 1948–49, it threatened to disrupt Lebanon's delicate demographic balance even though the vast majority of Palestinians were not granted citizenship (a policy that is still in place). Along with this greater Palestinian presence, there also existed outside interests in Lebanon, including the United States, Syria, Israel, the Soviet Union, and Iran. During the war, however, not everybody's loyalties followed party or religious lines. Some Christians "crossed over" and worked with Muslims, both Lebanese and Palestinian, a reality that has played a central role in Arab American fiction dealing with the war. The Phalange, the most powerful Maronite Christian militia, often relied on the support of Syrian Muslims. And Muslims themselves dealt with a variety of internecine problems. The Lebanese Civil War was a remarkably complicated affair, and even if we cannot comprehend the extent of its complexity, we should be aware of it. Such awareness prepares us to grasp the complexity of the Arab American literature that explores or takes place during the Lebanese Civil War.

Authors who represent the Lebanese Civil War generally explore the sectarian divides in Lebanon, in particular those between Maronite Christians and Palestinian Muslims. This sort of theme is unsurprising. People of Lebanese background make up a substantial portion of the Arab American community, and many Lebanese American writers lived through the war or have parents and other family who did. Representations of the Lebanese Civil War are an integral feature of the Arab American literary tradition. Writers such as Etel Adnan, Rawi Hage, and Patricia Sarrafian Ward have illuminated the nuances of the war for Western audiences.

Etel Adnan: Sexuality, Worldliness, and Humanism

Etel Adnan is one of the most recognizable writers of Arab origin in the world. Known mainly for her poetry, Adnan has also been successful in the genres of visual art and fiction. Her only novel, *Sitt Marie Rose,* has generated a significant audience and critical accolades. I focus on that novel here. First published in French by Des Femmes Paris in 1978, *Sitt Marie Rose* was translated into English in 1982 and issued by the independent Post-Apollo Press, where it has been the press's biggest seller. Although it might seem strange that a novel written in French falls into the category of "Arab American literature," in reality *Sitt Marie Rose* is a foundational text of modern Arab American fiction and Adnan one of the Arab American community's great advocates. Some of the literature written by Americans, it bears pointing out, has been done in languages other than English.

Adnan's personal diversity corresponds with the range of her artistic interests. A secularist born in Lebanon to a Syrian Muslim father and a Greek mother, Adnan is a transglobal person, living in northern California, Paris, and Beirut. This background has influenced her emphasis on transgression (the crossing of both physical and mental borders). The politics of Adnan's writing are focused on social issues in the Arab world, such as gender and sectarianism. Her aesthetics resemble the style of European modernism, in which nonlinear structures and multiple perspectives create a more intense and complex reading experience.

In terms of philosophy, Adnan often uses a humanist ethic in all aspects of her writing. This ethic is evident in *Sitt Marie Rose*. Adnan's literary and philosophical humanism resembles the themes and structures that French, British, and American writers explored throughout the greater part of the twentieth century. Humanism describes a worldview that sometimes appears in art and at other times in politics. It is a belief in the basic equality of all humans across cultures and religions. This description is narrow, but it intends to convey the spirit of humanistic ethos, which does not accept hierarchies based on identity or affiliation. A humanistic ethos would instead value a notion of inherent equality among humans and eschew any form of sectarian conflict (for instance, a civil conflict based on racial or religious identity).

Adnan's use of a humanistic ethos is particularly important in the context of her focus on Lebanon, a country with a history of sectarianism that led to civil war. That ethos allows her to criticize the various sectarian players in Lebanon from both moral and political standpoints. She does not confine her stylistic range to modernism and humanism, though; she also explores violence and sexuality as they intersect with a host of sociopolitical issues in the Middle East. One of the most conspicuous themes in *Sitt Marie Rose* is the conflation of sexual aggression with jingoism (a form of extreme patriotism that often manifests itself in aggression). The jingoism she condemns is related to the sort of religious-ethnic identity she opposes.

Beyond the themes of sexuality and humanism, much of Adnan's work is concerned with worldliness, a fact evident in *Sitt Marie Rose*. The term *worldliness* means many things depending on the context in which it is used. It can mean "sophisticated" or "knowledgeable" or "well traveled." In literary studies, it embodies all three of these descriptors, but it refers to something more specific: the recognition of cultures and practices beyond one's own worldview or experience. This recognition enables the literary critic to extricate herself from parochial readings and view literature as being engaged with numerous ideas and places in the world. The Palestinian American literary critic Edward Said, who developed the notion of critical worldliness in the 1970s, describes *worldliness* as "another term for secularism, again in opposition to the religious."[1] Said's mention of "the religious" is meant to condemn any dogmatism that leads readers and critics to be narrow-minded or even chauvinistic (an attitude of zealotry or excessive bias). He prefers instead that readers move beyond dogma and into other worlds of understanding.

Such a way of reading facilitates interpretation of *Sitt Marie Rose* because Adnan writes so adamantly against narrow religious understandings of the world. Although the novel is short, resembling a novella, it presents challenges because it is multivocal and does not always adhere to linear time. Set in 1976, it is broken into two sections, "Time I: A Million Birds" and "Time II: Marie-Rose," the latter in turn containing three sections, with seven brief chapters in each. "Time I" uses an unnamed narrator, or overnarrator, whose exact identity is never revealed but who appears to be a woman. "Time II" uses multiple points of view in the following sequence:

1. The children
2. Marie-Rose
3. Mounir
4. Tony
5. Fouad
6. Bouna Lias
7. The overnarrator

Mounir, Tony, Fouad, and Bouna Lias belong to the Phalangist militia (the Phalange Party), a largely Maronite Christian group. (Maronites are an Eastern Rite Catholic sect and make up the majority of Lebanon's Christian population.) The

Phalangists were major players in the Lebanese Civil War, implicated in a number of massacres. Arab American writers, whether Muslim or Christian, universally condemn them as belligerent agitators.

This sort of perspective has created some controversy around *Sitt Marie Rose*, which portrays the *chabab*—literally "young men," but used as in "the crew" or "the boys"—as sexually deviant and violently aggressive, two qualities that are not unrelated. *Sitt Marie Rose* is unavailable in Beirut because of its purported anti-Christian bias, which seems like a good place to start in examining the novel. Accusations that Adnan has an anti-Christian bias are probably unfair, but *Sitt Marie Rose* certainly portrays members of the Phalange negatively by highlighting the violence that existed in the movement. There is no need to hide from the fact that Adnan implicates political Christianity in that violence. However, it is important to note that she is also critical of Muslims. Her criticisms of both religions exist in the context of her displeasure with religious discourse's ability to become chauvinistic. This sort of criticism forms one of the central themes of *Sitt Marie Rose*.

In fact, the other seminal themes around gender and sexuality are closely related to Adnan's secular humanism. The *chabab* possess a sexual deviancy that underlines their callousness. One expression of their callousness or lack of empathy occurs in "Time I," where Mounir describes the pleasures of hunting to the disapproving overnarrator. The overnarrator immediately notices the presence of guns: "The hunting rifles are clearly in view."[2] These rifles are symbolic of machismo, an attitude that can be performed through supposedly "manly" pursuits that are inevitably violent. The attitude also weakens the *chabab*'s sense of empathy: "None of them has ever found in a woman the same sensation of power he gets from a car. An auto rally is more significant than a conjugal night, and hunting is better still" (3). Adnan includes issues of class in this character profile; "Mounir's family is extremely rich," the overnarrator observes, which allows Mounir to pursue his "projects and distractions" (2–3). Fouad, another member of the *chabab*, "hunts as though obsessed. He prefers killing to kissing. He hates the expression 'to make love' because you don't make anything, as he says. He prefers jeep-speed-desert-bird-bullet to girl-in-a-bed-and-fuck" (2).

Here, Adnan combines machismo, sexual aggression, class, and violence in the personas of characters who supposedly form the core of this society's respectability. In other words, the *chabab* consider themselves to be normative (something that is normative represents or is said to represent the desirable or mainstream values of any given community). Adnan therefore exposes a violence embedded in the core of a purportedly civilized society. Fouad in particular embodies sexual dysfunction and political belligerence. He prefers guns and cars to women, but his relationship with those objects is nevertheless markedly sexual. Killing provides him a lustful relief. Although other members of the *chabab* are not so explicitly vicious, they share a fundamental outlook with Fouad, who merely vocalizes something that remains hidden beneath the veneer of gentility within the others. The overnarrator explains, "They are moved by a sick sexuality, a mad love, where images of crushing and cries dominate" (66). This "sick sexuality" is indivisible from their chauvinism; in many ways, the sick sexuality foregrounds it.

Another troublesome quality of the *chabab* is their Eurocentric outlook. Of the *chabab*, for instance, Marie-Rose observes, "These young boys were exalted by the Crusades" (47). The Crusades were a series of military conquests in the Middle Ages wherein Europeans invaded the Middle East in order to recapture Jerusalem from the "infidels" (Muslims). The Crusades were remarkably violent and led to legendary battles and horrifying bloodshed. Extended European occupations of parts of the Middle East have become integral to the modern identities of Turks, Syrians, Lebanese, Palestinians, and Jordanians. Light-skinned or light-haired Arabs are often referred to as having "Crusader blood." Although the Crusades are viewed in the United States largely as just another historical epoch, they are an enormous part of the cultural imagination of people in the Middle East. Adnan invokes the Crusades, then, to cast light on the psychology of the *chabab*; their fascination with the Crusades renders them unmistakably negative characters, prone to self-hatred and racist violence.

In fact, the *chabab*'s Eurocentric outlook not only fuels their violence, but also in their minds simultaneously justifies it. By admiring the Crusades and outfitting themselves with an imagined European identity, the *chabab* position themselves as modern in opposition to their Muslim counterparts, whom they view as premodern or barbaric. The *chabab* have entered into modernity, which renders them civilized and in their eyes normative. Political modernity does not necessarily describe an actual condition as much as it describes a state of mind— or, to be more precise, a self-made state of mind. In many ways, modernity is an attitude that a community confers on itself, as the *chabab* do in *Sitt Marie Rose*.

In very crude terms, it can be seen as a coded description of civility as opposed to the savagery that exists in the Third World, Islamic countries in particular.

Political scientist Mahmood Mamdani has examined how modernity and violence interact. "The modern sensibility is not horrified by pervasive violence," he observes. "The world wars are proof enough of this. What horrifies our modern sensibility is violence that appears senseless, that cannot be justified by progress."[3] Mamdani's formulation describes the *chabab*'s attitude perfectly. They view their violence, however vicious, as moral and necessary, even divinely inspired—the Crusaders and their many apologists in later centuries did the same thing, as did the colonizers who ravaged the Southern Hemisphere in more recent times. The *chabab* dismiss the violence of their Muslim enemies as irrational lunacy from which the goodness they represent must be protected. This type of justification for violence—which never actually presents itself as violent—is part and parcel of political modernity, a reality that *Sitt Marie Rose* examines in detail. Mounir, for instance, notes, "It's violence that accelerates the progress of a people" (55).

Adnan's humanistic leanings compel her to cast such a reality in a negative light. She does so primarily by detailing the *chabab*'s irrationality, illuminating the ugliness of their violence, and setting up a counterweight, in the character of Marie-Rose, to their self-identity as protectors of civility. Marie-Rose acts as a moral arbiter in the novel in two main ways: by limiting the force of the *chabab*'s narratives and by providing an unflagging decency amid the worst of human behavior. The overnarrator describes her as "a blade of grass in the bulldozer's path" (104), a metaphor indicating that the *chabab* are possessed of a bloodlust that must be satiated, although conferring to Marie-Rose a certain power because even after being run over by a bulldozer a blade of grass will not be eradicated or uprooted. In her running dialogue with Mounir, once an object of her youthful affection, Marie-Rose refuses to concede to him any moral ground, even when he purports to be interested in helping her. She recognizes this so-called generosity as a political maneuver.

Marie-Rose, then, is shrewd in addition to morally astute. Adnan highlights her many positive qualities through a recurring metaphor, the Virgin Mary. This metaphor reflects Marie-Rose's desire to cross boundaries in that the immaculate conception is accepted by both Christians and Muslims (who revere Jesus as a prophet second in importance to Muhammad). Her name, of course, is the first use of the metaphor, which Adnan reinforces through the reverent children's point of view: "[Marie-Rose] looks like the Blessed Virgin at church, the big one, the one that stares at us during mass" (45). Her resemblance to the Virgin is not merely behavioral; it is also physical. Adnan uses this sort of heavy-handed imagery in order to create an interaction of conflicting narratives. She does not implicate Maronite Christianity, which Marie-Rose views as fundamentally liberatory; rather, she implicates the sectarian attitude that permeates many of its practitioners. Religion is not completely guilty in *Sitt Marie Rose*. The novel does not represent an atheist tract. It instead re-creates the biblical fall of man through his fallacy, with the *chabab* playing the role of the corrupted and Marie-Rose the ideal of the pure. The deaf-mute children, for example, claim that "she never does anything bad, Marie-Rose" (81).

It is because of Marie-Rose's purity that the *chabab* are so enraged by her supposed indiscretions. Extending the motif of sexual dysfunction, the *chabab*— the ostensibly rational Mounir in particular—are perturbed by Marie-Rose's relationship with a Palestinian Muslim physician who is active in leftist politics. Tony makes his feelings about the relationship explicit: "She should not have had a Palestinian for a friend. She could have found someone better to sleep with" (60). Tony does not appear to mind Marie-Rose's sexual activity per se, but rather her choice of sexual partner. He cannot tolerate her sleeping with the enemy, in his mind a backward presence in an otherwise civilized land. His infatuation with violence and his medieval ethos are thus ironic. In the *chabab*'s mind, Marie-Rose is a symbol not only of purity, but of their salvation, something they own like a possession; thus, by giving her body to the hated enemy, she has violated their illusion of chastity and their confidence in the rightness of their cause.

The character Bouna Lias, a Maronite priest and apparently a high-ranking member of the clergy, provides a more interesting reaction to Marie-Rose's relationship. (*Bouna* is the title for priests in the Arab world, translating literally to "Our Father" and usually transliterated as "Abuna.") He admonishes her with reference to the symbolic importance of her name: "Your soul is going to sink, Marie-Rose, you who bear the name of both the Virgin and her symbol. Families will speak of you and your treason for a long time to come, and without mercy" (96–97). Bouna Lias is there to provide legitimacy to the *chabab*'s violence, and in this way he is a metonymical character (metonymy is the use of one object to represent a related or broader object). He represents the church's complicity in organizing and validating sectarian conflict. He is the authoritative presence that absolves the *chabab* of their brutality and confers to them the illusion of divinity. His interpersonal kindness, then, is actually a smokescreen for fascistic politics.

The Palestinian doctor in turn also assumes a symbolic importance, highlighted by the fact that readers never actually meet him. The *chabab* view his corruption of Marie-Rose as emblematic of the unwanted Palestinian refugee presence in Lebanon: just as the doctor has soured Marie-Rose's purity, so have the Palestinians sullied an otherwise idyllic Lebanon. (Literary scholars refer to this sort of thinking as nostalgia, a romanticized view of the past that does not usually conform to the reality of what is being remembered.) The doctor has taken something that they feel is rightly theirs; this viewpoint combines sexism with chauvinism and reveals the inherent contradictions of sectarianism: an action is considered to be immoral not on its own merits, but based on its loyalty to a particular group. Mounir, for instance, cites the importance of loyalty as a justification for keeping Marie-Rose captive: "I'm their friend, it's true, but I'm also their section chief. I can't say no to my comrades" (33).

This need to instill loyalty, however misguided, inspires the *chabab*'s ghastly decision to torture and kill Marie-Rose in front of the deaf-mute children. As Fouad says, "And these children keep wanting to go out. Deaf and mute they're lost from the start. But we want them to stay. We want them to see what happens to traitors. Sitt-Marie Rose? She conned them all right, this Sitt-Marie Rose. They'll have to see with their own eyes what's going to happen to her. They must learn so that later they won't get any ideas about rebellion. You never know, nowadays, even deaf-mutes could become subversives" (61). The deaf-mute children are made to bear witness to Marie-Rose's execution, a fact that emphasizes their ability to see. This bit of symbolism can be interpreted in different ways. On the one hand, it has the practical effect of allowing the *chabab* to force the children to bear witness to torture and execution, a morbid way to obtain their loyalty. On the other hand, the fact that they bear witness to Marie-Rose's execution allows them to play a narrative role by conjoining the story of Marie-Rose to the reader's consciousness. They see for the reader; the reader can then hear and speak for them.

Adnan's political criticisms move beyond the condemnation of the *chabab*. She situates the Lebanese Civil War in the context of the Arab world, whose politics have contributed to historical strife in Lebanon. At one point, Marie-Rose complains, "The Arab world is infinitely large in terms of space and infinitely small in its vision. It's made up of sects and sub-sects, ghettoes, communities, worked by envy, rotten, closed back on themselves like worms" (57). This pessimism, articulated during an argument with Fouad, belies Marie-Rose's history as an advocate for the poor and oppressed—indeed, as a harbinger of goodwill and justice. We must examine the statement within the framework of that history, then. Marie-Rose is performing a specific rhetorical act, one that admonishes Lebanese sectarianism by condemning fragmentation in the Arab world in general. In this sense, she is critical neither of Maronites nor of Muslims as much as she is frustrated by Arabs' failure to unite across cultural, national, and religious lines. This desire is a basic feature of the humanism evident in *Sitt Marie Rose*. It manifests itself specifically in the criticism of Arab Muslims for their failure to bring about the liberation of Palestinians.

It would be tempting to speculate that Marie-Rose acts as a mouthpiece for Adnan's own viewpoints, but I am a bit wary of searching for autobiography in literary characters. Even if certain connections between an author and character are obvious, looking for such connections does not necessarily constitute the most productive way to read and respond to a novel. It is more useful to consider the characters' place within the textual worlds they inhabit and in the larger world within which the text exists. It is probably safe to say that Marie-Rose endeavors to represent the potential for good that exists in humanity, whereas the *chabab* encompass a failed morality of sectarianism and divisiveness. Although *Sitt Marie Rose* takes place in Lebanon, the novel provides a relevant theme for all humankind, one that emphasizes our common humanity more than our superficial differences. Marie-Rose is the humanist inside everybody, even those who have embraced their baser instincts.

Rawi Hage: Unearthing Beirut's Dangerous Games

Unlike most of the writers featured in this book, Rawi Hage is not technically an "Arab American." He is a citizen of Canada, originally from Lebanon, although he lived in the United States during his teenage years. Hage's first novel, *De Niro's Game*, was a critical success upon its publication in Canada and received favorable reviews when it was released in the United States, later winning the prestigious Dublin Impact Award. Although, as with all other novels, many different themes are worthy of exploration in this novel, I focus here on Hage's representations of the Lebanese Civil War and its various uses in the narrative.

De Niro's Game is a linear story told from the point of view of Bassam Al-Abyad, a Christian resident of East Beirut (the "Christian side"). The novel is noteworthy for its use of elaborate, descriptive language, often resulting in long sentences, a technique that modernists such as William Faulkner developed. Hage also uses oblique rather than explicit description to convey action such as deaths and violent confrontations, a move that creates an intriguing and compelling narrative. Also noteworthy is Hage's minimalist approach to dialogue, which, rather than being set into quotation marks, is inscribed in the regular narrative. This style produces a less formal but more intense reading experience by challenging the audience to invest themselves in conversations with the same commitment they devote to the narrator. Another interesting feature of the novel is the fact that unlike *Sitt Marie Rose*, *De Niro's Game* has no clear "good" or "bad" characters. Although the novel takes place mainly in a Christian community and features a large proportion of Christian characters, Christianity and Islam are not set apart from one another; Hage carefully avoids binaries. Readers are introduced to a wide variety of political viewpoints and ethical commitments even among the Christian characters themselves.

These gray areas are reflected vividly in one scene in which Christian and Muslim soldiers shoot at one another partly in jest and partly in seriousness. They have developed a rapport that came into existence based not only on their proximity across the Green Line (the unofficial border between East and West Beirut), but on the frequency with which they are called to hold their positions. The dividing line is never as strong as the basic human impulses that traverse it. The Christian militiamen are even on a first-name basis with one of the Muslim soldiers, Hassan, and joke with him in a harsh but friendly manner. Hassan returns the favor: "When everyone stopped shooting we heard Hassan's voice from the other side. He shouted something about a prostitute, about Christian mothers. Everyone laughed."[4] One of the soldiers later explains to a slightly surprised Bassam, "We promised each other that when this war ends we will have a drink" (55). Despite the divisiveness in Lebanon that led to and results from the civil war, the Lebanese still retain an inherent sense of cohesiveness as compatriots who share a history and a national culture.

In *De Niro's Game*, though, the war has corrupted the Lebanese. Bassam wastes no time setting a mood for his story: "War is for thugs. Motorcycles are also for thugs, and for longhaired teenagers like us, with guns under our bellies, and stolen gas in our tanks, and no particular place to go" (13). He goes on: "We were aimless, beggars and thieves, horny Arabs with curly hair and open shirts and Marlboro packs rolled in our sleeves, dropouts, ruthless nihilists with guns, bad breath, and long American jeans" (13). These colorful descriptions create a sense that people have been corrupted, but they nevertheless draw readers into the lives of fascinating characters. This type of description culminates with Bassam's tart response to a child soldier who detains him at a checkpoint and accuses him of stealing: "We are all thieves in this war, I said" (41). Hage's portrait of Beirut is reminiscent of the description provided by the British journalist Robert Fisk, who has observed that Beirut's "hopelessness relies upon its resilience. There are those who praise the courage of its people, their valour amid despair, but it is this very capacity for survival, for eternal renewal, that is Beirut's tragedy."[5]

It would be a mistake, however, to call *De Niro's Game* nihilistic (nihilism is a feeling characterized by a rejection of reality or a sense of nothingness). It is better described as realistic, with the characters responding to extremely difficult living conditions by engaging in behavior indicative of a breakdown of moral values, which in turn is a result of the breakdown of Lebanon's tenuous social structure. One major aspect of the novel in this vein concerns the collapse of the nuclear family, exemplified by the theme of the absent father. Bassam's best friend, George, is fatherless, a fact that everybody seems to be silently aware of and that George never acknowledges: "He never mentioned his father. The word was that his father was a Frenchman who had come to our land, planted a seed in his mother's young womb, and flown back north like a migrating bird" (34). George is not the only character without a father present: Bassam's unnamed father is conspicuously absent; Bassam indicates that his father was a degenerate gambler and an alcoholic. The theme of absent fathers has been used consistently in Western art forms, both visual and literary, so Hage is not producing something entirely original. The originality in his use of this theme lies in the fact that he contextualizes it with expressions of male lust and violence stemming from that lust.

The origin of George's unknown father comes to play a huge role in the novel's plot. In the third part of *De Niro's Game*, the novel transitions into something of a spy thriller, a surprising turn that alters not only the setting of the novel (from Beirut to Paris), but also its tempo and tone. It turns out that George's father was a Frenchman of Jewish origin who ranked highly in the Mossad

(Israel's spy agency). George, too, it turns out, had been working for the Mossad before his death, not a complete surprise given his open collaboration with Israel (something some of the Christian militias did during the civil war). These revelations reinforce many of the implications that arose earlier through the theme of the absent father, in particular Bassam and George's rootlessness and the chaos of upheaval that ensues during times of war. There is nothing certain that can be used to center the world any longer.

The culmination of this chaos and violence occurs shortly before George's death, when readers learn that he has taken part in the Sabra and Shatila massacre—a massacre undertaken in 1982 against Palestinian civilians in the Shatila Refugee Camp, just south of Beirut, and in the adjoining neighborhood of Sabra, heavily Palestinian, when Maronite forces under the supervision of Israeli soldiers entered into the area and over the course of three days slaughtered anywhere from fifteen hundred to three thousand people, nearly all of them unarmed. The massacre ended up receiving international news coverage and resulted in a political scandal inside Israel. A drunk and drugged George explains to Bassam, "We attacked a Palestinian camp and killed by the hundreds, maybe thousands" (174). George implicates Israel in the massacre, noting that an Israeli liaison officer and Abou-Nahra, a Phalange militia commander, delivered the following injunction: "We have to purify the camps" (174).

This choice of language is revealing. By using the word *purify*, Hage makes a number of allusions that highlight some of the novel's important moral positions and ground it in actual historical events. The most striking allusion is to the Nazis, who were fond of the word *purify* and the concept it signified in their program of eugenics (a movement supposedly to improve the human gene pool by eliminating "undesirables" such as the disabled, the mentally retarded, and members of "inferior" races). Historians have implicated some of the Phalange leaders for their admiration of Nazi beliefs and strategies. Another allusion of note is to the sectarian belief that the name "Lebanese" describes only somebody of a proper background racially, culturally, religiously, and economically. Literary critics refer to this sort of thinking as reductionism—that is, reducing something, such as an identity, to a narrow set of criteria that only a limited number of people can claim (narrowing an identity like this thus works in the interests of the group that developed the criteria in the first place). The Palestinians are decidedly not Lebanese, so they must be cleansed for the sake of

Lebanon's rightful inhabitants (who, according to the subtext, are also upper class and Christian).

Here is one of the few points at which *De Niro's Game* resembles *Sitt Marie Rose*. Although both novels are set amid the Lebanese Civil War, they are quite different stylistically and structurally (and sometimes philosophically). However, both novels examine the interrelation of wartime violence with sexual aggression. Bassam avoids joining the militia, but his character combines an internal anger with frequent lust, which he often acts on by making sexual advances on (and ultimately sleeping with) George's aunt Nabila. George, the militiaman, is a more obvious embodiment of sexual aggression, as when he boasts to fellow militiamen of his conquest of a married woman, Nicole, whose husband, Laurent, encourages their exploits. The story elicits the following reaction from one of the soldiers: "I would fuck them both, yelled Abou-Haddid. And the maid too" (96). As the novel develops, Nicole increasingly has illicit sex and a worsening drug addiction, and Laurent eagerly and almost manically enables her habits.

On one level, the couple become emblematic of the breakdown of Lebanese society. They more profoundly, though, come to signify a yearning for something from the past that is now gone, something that is never coming back, something that in any case never actually existed but was merely imagined in the present. When Bassam asks Laurent why he spoils and enables Nicole, Laurent tells a story about the Lebanese merchant class in Africa that acted as a liaison for colonial France. To Laurent, those supposed glory days, notwithstanding the exploitation of local Africans, represent a city on the hill, the very essence of Lebanon's appeal. "And all I am trying to do is spend my last days close to that hill," he explains (123). He has been broken by the same fantasy George wishes to restore.

Even though *De Niro's Game* is linear and tells a story filled with action, the novel's strength relies on its complex symbology (a system of symbols or a way of describing the use of symbolism). The title itself reflects George's nickname, "De Niro," which comes from the famous American actor and appears to be used mainly as his nom de guerre (military name). Bassam, who narrates the novel, refers to him as "George," and Nabila refers to him with the childlike nickname "Gargourty." But it is in the name "De Niro" that most of the character's power lies. Hage uses a bit of pastiche to render the name central to a crucial plot development. (Pastiche most often describes a book or movie that consciously references, alludes to, or reconceptualizes a prior work of art. It also describes a mixing of styles and genres in order to undermine conventional storytelling norms. *De Niro's Game* adheres to the first definition.) At the end of part two, an unstable George threatens to imprison Bassam, who has already been locked up and tortured for supposedly killing Laurent and stealing his diamonds, though his captors care only about the whereabouts of the diamonds. Instead of taking Bassam to the torture chamber, however, George parks his car underneath a bridge.

Readers soon learn that George's nickname is not merely happenstance as he proceeds to act out a scene for which De Niro is famous. Hage offers a pastiche of the 1979 film *The Deer Hunter* in which De Niro and his friends are taken as prisoners of war in Vietnam and forced to play roulette with live ammunition while their captors gamble. The game continues until one of the two contestants has shot himself in the temple. In *The Deer Hunter,* roulette functions as the epitome of both violence and despair, a function that Hage reproduces in *De Niro's Game.* Under the influence of drugs and with a partially loaded revolver in his hand, George makes a deal with Bassam: "No, Bassam, the torture chambers are inside us. But I am fair, and you are my brother. I will give you a way out, De Niro said" (179). This passage is interesting because it marks the only time in Bassam's narration that he refers to George as "De Niro," signifying that an irreversible transformation has occurred and that George's prophesy has been fulfilled. It also signals a complete breakdown of Lebanon's social fabric, mirrored by the disintegration of George and Bassam's friendship into violence. The scene ends ambiguously. Readers learn later that George lost the game of roulette and shot his brains onto his car windshield. (In *Koolaids: The Art of War,* Rabih Alameddine also depicts Lebanese soldiers playing roulette. See chapter 4.)

Roulette may be the obvious "game" indicated by the novel's title, but it is not the only one. Hage's character De Niro plays many games, the most notable one being a scheme he devises with Bassam in order to siphon money from a casino run by the militia. This scheme immediately signals to readers that Hage will not adhere to any traditional binary fixated on good and evil characters. Instead, readers are presented with characters who are morally complex and sometimes act immorally at least partly in response to the chaos in which they exist. War itself is often referred to as a "game," and it seems reasonable to speculate that Hage has this usage in mind, particularly as a way of drawing attention to the dishonesty inherent in political movements. The word *game,* in any case, matches well with the characters' complex morality: if everything is a game, then the incentive to behave responsibly wanes if it does not dissipate altogether.

De Niro's Game puts forward this type of realistic message without ever becoming pedantic. In fact, the novel's structure ensures that the disorder underlying the Lebanese Civil War will be reflected in the characters' complicated actions. Everybody, from Nabila to Rhea, challenges the typical categories of morality and behavior that readers often expect of major and minor characters (expectations usually based on age, ethnicity, religion, and gender). Even the most consistent bit of symbolism in the novel, the repetition of the number ten thousand, seems to have no discernible meaning. At the very least, it does not have a consistent usage in terms of where and in which conditions Hage employs it. The number may represent a death count, a period of time, or some sort of cultural or political numerology. Because the story does not offer us an indication of what the number alludes to external of the novel, then we can examine it within the context of the story itself. The repetition of this number has its own logic within *De Niro's Game,* most obviously in the fact that in the first two sections the number never describes anything joyous, only things that are to varying degrees tragic: bombs, cigarettes, needles, whisky, civilian deaths. In the third part, it describes items that are more mundane: fish, waves, and cars, though it also references creatures, devils, and the pieces of shattered windshield glass, which the narrator calls "glowing red-and-green diamonds" (272).

However, Hage uses the number ten thousand most often to describe bombs falling, an image that he repeats throughout the novel. The image and the accompanying number, then, permeate the story as an inextricable part of its setting. And because Hage repeats the number in a variety of other descriptions, it appears that bombs are the reference point from which all other actions emanate. The war is not only the novel's crucial setting, but also its most influential character. It has the ability to affect all the other characters with a power that they are lacking. Not even the French characters can avoid the reach of the war. The only thing that seems to be outside of its influence is the city of Rome, which Bassam has rendered something of an abstract fantasy. The novel closes as he buys a train ticket from Paris to Rome. The scene symbolizes the possibility of an escape, even if readers never learn for certain whether Bassam arrives there safely. It is the dream of the escape that is most important.

It is indicative of the novel's complexity that Hage chooses to end *De Niro's Game* on what might be a note of hopefulness or at least of serenity. Everything that leads to Bassam's purchase of a train ticket to Rome gives readers the impression that war is inescapable and that basic human goodness is a myth. Such features help make the novel intriguing and compelling because Hage expertly pulls readers toward the characters. This move is not a matter of asking (or forcing) readers to identify with the characters, but one of asking (or forcing) us to recognize our own flawed human tendencies as they are reflected in the characters' actions. As Bassam points out, "Many had died playing De Niro's game" (231).

Patricia Sarrafian Ward: The Mental Paraphernalia of War

I start here again with technical commentary: Patricia Sarrafian Ward is not an Arab, but she usually is classified as an "Arab American writer." She was born in Lebanon to a Lebanese father of Armenian origin and a white American mother. Armenians have long had a presence in the Arab world and live in countries such as Lebanon, Syria, Jordan, Palestine, and Egypt. Although maintaining their own language and sense of history as an ethnic community, Armenians have also integrated culturally and economically into the societies in which they live. Mainly Orthodox Christian, the Armenians of Lebanon did not stake out a particular position during the civil war and were noted for their lack of explicit sectarianism.

Ward belongs in an analysis of Arab American literature for a few reasons. She participates in the Arab American literary community—that is to say, she contributes writing to Arab American publications, attends gatherings focused on Arab American literature, and is a well-known member of the Arab American arts community. Her work is also found on syllabi and reading lists focused on Arab American writing. Beyond Ward's personal decisions, it is useful to think about the position of Armenian minorities in the Arab world. Although Armenians are not ethnic Arabs, they are integral to Middle Eastern histories and inseparable from any contemporary notion of Lebanese culture. You may encounter Ward's *The Bullet Collection* in your Arab American literature course because it deals in part with the Middle East and is written by somebody with a background native to the region.

If you find that *The Bullet Collection* somehow reads differently than a typical novel, then try not to fret. One of its noteworthy qualities is the fact that

Ward creates a distinctive reading experience. Rather than employing a didactic style like Adnan's or a fast-moving, suspenseful one like Hage's, Ward writes in a patient fashion, developing symbolic phenomena that ultimately compose the primary content of the novel. *The Bullet Collection* is the type of book I like to call a "reader's novel"—a novel that one must read slowly and carefully in order to understand and appreciate its considerable artistry. It is best read with an emphasis on its symbolism and with an eye toward what happens in the background as it influences the characters' trajectories and behavior.

The Bullet Collection focuses on a nuclear family—parents Stephen and Ani, daughters Marianna and Magdalaine (Alaine)—that has arrived in New England from war-torn Lebanon. Stephen is an American-born history professor who worked at Beirut's prestigious American University; Ani is a Lebanese-born Armenian. Although the novel is told from the point of view of Marianna, the younger sister, one can argue that its main protagonist is Alaine because Marianna focuses so much of her narration on her observations of Alaine, illuminating how Alaine plays a central role physically and symbolically in her nuclear family and in both Lebanon and the United States. Alaine is largely a silent character whose voice often arises through actions that worry her family, such as collecting war debris and searching out dead bodies, behavior that does not intimate morbidity as much as a physical manifestation of memory and a devotion to survival: "Alaine whispered, Come into my room, and she put whatever she had found into my hands—a sock, a bloodstained tie, eyeglasses—and gave me warnings. Don't go out alone. Don't talk to anyone you don't know. Don't argue with anyone."[6]

Indeed, Alaine evinces a mysterious quality, but readers do not get a clear indication that she is an insane or unreliable character. When she tells Marianna that she is "smarter than Huda" or has "things to do" (85), it is difficult to question either her sincerity or sense of purpose. Alaine is on some sort of antidepressant medication, so Ward does indicate that to some degree she is troubled. However, we miss the richness of Alaine's character if we ascribe her choices to mental or emotional instability. They are better understood in the context of the civil war's effect on social and interpersonal stability, a theme Hage explores in *De Niro's Game* with the disintegration of George and Bassam's moral values. Alaine does not represent a fall into immorality, though; she reflects a social upheaval arising from the presence of immoral warfare. She collects the physical effects of warfare as a way of signifying its emotional realities.

The novel's main themes revolve around these emotional realities, especially dislocation, alienation, and exile. Many famous authors, including Edward Said, Chinua Achebe, and Jhumpa Lahiri, have written about what exile means and what it means to be in exile. I would add *The Bullet Collection* to the long and distinguished list of literary works that explore a separation from home by looking at the emotional and physical effects of emigration or displacement. The primary characters in *The Bullet Collection* are dislocated, and they are burdened by that dislocation in most dimensions of their daily lives. Perhaps a better word to describe their condition would be *alienation*. That alienation is reflected in Ward's meticulous, sometimes haunting descriptions. About their house, for instance, Marianna notes, "We live in a green wood house on a lump of hill, patchy grass falling away on either side. The house sags in the center, as if the earth wants to reclaim it from the surface" (58). The "lump" on which the unstable house sits reflects an increased visibility and incompleteness, as if there is more to come and the house knows it, waiting for the earth to swallow its dour and unnatural existence. Even Marianna's physical traits are indicative of an exilic existence; she laments the fact that because of her mixed parentage she is often seen as foreign in both Lebanon and the United States.

The descriptions of people are no more cheerful. Marianna: "My face in the bathroom mirror: blotchy, pale skin. Dry and chafed red around the nose and between the eyebrows, a skin condition that worsens in this American cold" (60). Marianna's father finds life back in the United States burdensome: "His face had grown too thin, grown deep lines around the mouth, across the forehead, and now he looked to the side, tapping his cigarette on the ashtray with nothing more to say" (60). Marianna's mother has an interesting perspective on this sad and lonely condition: "We are, Mummy explained, a quintessential American family, come here from strife and ready to make a new future" (60). This statement, which Marianna has a difficult time believing, underscores a set of important historical truths about the United States. It is certainly a country to which people come and continue to come in order to escape strife. The mother, however, highlights the strife that many immigrants continue to face in the United States, where the promise of success and comfort is more easily imagined than achieved. Yet her comment, in acknowledging that America is also a place to escape strife, contains an implicit hopefulness, a belief that in America life is supposed to improve. Marianna does not believe her mother because her mother is still stuck on the dream and has not moved on to the reality.

In feeling trapped by a dour life in New England, Marianna has a tendency to remember Lebanon with a certain nostalgia despite the violence of the war from which her family has escaped. In the novel, this nostalgia is sometimes articulated through the phrase "Lebanon magic," a way to quantify Lebanon's specialness. As the narrative progresses, Marianna gradually loses her faith in the strength and even existence of Lebanon magic, realizing that it has mostly been constructed in the present rather than being an accurate remembrance of the past. The magical Lebanon contrasts with the bleakness of the present in New England. Most anything can become magical in such circumstances. More important, for Marianna Lebanon becomes a default space against which other spaces can be judged, and her memories of a home country reveal a lapse between perception and reality. This lapse is an important symbolic theme throughout the novel and is rendered explicit when Marianna's mother observes, "You can't argue with the way someone remembers things," complementing her husband's oblique comment, "The past is a code that may or may not be broken" (41).

This distance from the past is a quintessential American motif. Part of the allure of settlement in the so-called New World was the promise of a new beginning, the belief that America can facilitate the pursuit of a brighter future. This motif is not the only American discourse that Ward explores in *The Bullet Collection*. She also plays up the appeal of the United States as if it is enchanted: "America: This is the land where people want to be, that is what Mummy told me once. She said, You're living where half the world dreams of being" (271). A New England boring in its normalcy contrasts sharply with an edgy Lebanon, where war disrupts even the most mundane dimensions of life. Both Marianna and Alaine remember Lebanon fondly at times and want to return. Their father, vibrant and prominent in Lebanon, is only a shell of a human in New England. Even their mother, who dispenses American mythologies to her children, cannot escape Lebanon's appeal—the appeal of her past—despite the fact that she deems Lebanon magic "self-aggrandizement" (271). These contrasts endow the novel with a complex, sometimes haunting sense of place in which exile plays a seminal role in the characters' identities, preventing them from developing a cogent relationship either with the American polity or with their memories of Lebanon.

Such disjunctions are common in the Arab American writing that deals with the Lebanese Civil War. Although Adnan, Hage, and Ward offer works that differ in content and style, strongly in some cases, their novels do share some

noteworthy similarities. Hage and Ward, for example, employ comparable structures and emphasize some of the same themes. In *The Bullet Collection*, Ziad
plays Russian roulette, one of Hage's seminal images. Ward avoids the use of
quotation marks for her dialogue, as does Hage, which creates a similar tempo for
reading and has the same overall effect on the novel's aesthetics: drawing readers
into the narrative by removing the traditional structural markers that organize a
work of fiction. Despite these similarities, though, *The Bullet Collection* is unique,
offering its readers a transnational story that invests itself in Lebanon and the
United States without remaining confined to either.

Conclusion

The dynamics of migration and immigration play an enormous role in the development of American literature. (Literary critics, insofar as they make a distinction, generally view *migration* as an inevitable process of human movement based
on social and historical conditions and *immigration* as a more conscious decision
to settle elsewhere.) American literature is so exciting now, in fact, because it
reflects the movement of peoples across the globe into the United States as well
as the movement of Americans to places across the globe. As writers of Lebanese background have been published in English by American houses, Lebanon
comes to play a role in the American literary scene. If you are a reader of Adnan,
Hage, and Ward's works, then, the Lebanese Civil War has entered into your
consciousness, a transaction that defines the potential of literature to inform
and excite. Even though each writer employs a distinct aesthetic, their work does
share an important feature: the transportation of readers into a particular space
that is chaotic, violent, redeeming, and, finally, universal.

3

Exploring Islam(s) in America

Mohja Kahf

IN THE LATE 1990s, the distinguished scholar Mohja Kahf turned to creative writing, publishing the well-received poetry collection *Letters from Scheherazad*. A few years later, in 2006, Kahf released her first novel, *The Girl in the Tangerine Scarf*, which quickly went on to become one of the most critically and commercially successful Arab American novels. Before the publication of *The Girl in the Tangerine Scarf*, most Arab American novelists treated the culture and practice of Islam either tangentially or intermittently. In Kahf's novel, however, Islam is a primary theme, one that she explores as a highly diverse set of beliefs and customs.

Kahf's focus on Islam does not mean that she ignores issues of ethnicity. In fact, she represents several ethnic communities in addition to Arab Americans. The characters in the novel include an Orthodox Jew, an Arab Christian, and an American-born Hindu of South Asian origin. *The Girl in the Tangerine Scarf*, then, is a layered exploration of modern, multicultural America. One of the novel's effects is to complicate readers' perceptions of what elements compose the Muslim American community theologically and culturally. Kahf is one of the first American writers to explore fictively the practitioners of conservative Islam in the United States. Her scholarly background as an expert in the representations of Muslim women and Arabic literature is evident in the novel's structure and its many interpersonal conflicts. Kahf's main characters grow into more acceptant social agents while retaining their core religious devoutness.

The novel's main character is Khadra Shamy, an American born to Syrian immigrant parents, Wajdy and Ebtihaj. Told from Khadra's point of view, the novel begins with an adult Khadra returning to the community in which she was raised on the outskirts of Indianapolis, a small town called Simmonsville. Her family's life in Simmonsville revolves around the Dawah Center, an Islamic education and outreach office where Wajdy works as a coordinator for a low salary. As soon as she enters Indiana, Khadra begins flashing back to both happy and unhappy childhood memories involving her close African American friends, the siblings Hakim and Hanifa, and their collective dealings with local racists and xenophobes. The story then transitions into a traditional linear narrative charting Khadra's life as she grows from a child in Indiana into the person we meet as the novel opens, a successful journalist based in Philadelphia.

Kahf's writing style is usually straightforward, with a detailed use of description. At times, her prose can be playful or preachy, though the narrator's recognition of these qualities tempers them and prevents the novel's tone from becoming didactic. At other times, the prose is sardonic or even self-deprecating, a style that moderates the fundamental seriousness of the novel's subject-matter. Kahf is able to explore complex and sometimes controversial material with an inviting and engaging approach because of the amiable prose style she employs, including:

• Racism as a layered phenomenon, not only directed at American Muslims by non-Muslims, but existing within the Muslim community itself, particularly toward African Americans by immigrants;

• Crossing ethnic and religious boundaries, as exemplified by the interfaith and intercultural relationships that develop in the novel;

• A sometimes competing and sometimes harmonious relationship between conservative and moderate Muslims;

• Gender issues in Muslim communities; and

• The numerous conflicts that exist around the process of Muslim acculturation into the United States.

Racism and xenophobia enter into the story almost immediately, setting the tone for their thematic importance. Khadra's older brother, Eyad, gets into a shouting match with another neighborhood kid, Brian, who responds to Eyad's admonition to stop his bullying by proclaiming, "Fuck you, raghead."[1] Readers soon learn that the apple does not fall far from the tree. "ACCUSING MY CHILDREN—OFF MY PORCH—BACK WHERE YOU PEOPLE CAME FROM!" Brian's father, Vaughn, screams at Wajdy after Wajdy calmly knocks on his neighbor's door (6–7). Kahf's inclusion of this sort of inhospitality is a common move in much of the American literature that focuses on immigration, although different authors, of course, explore such inhospitality in different ways. As the literary critic Ali Behdad notes, "The myth of America as an asylum obscures the ideological underpinnings of the state and the political economy of immigration, as well as the importance of xenophobia in the founding of the United States."[2] Behdad points to the violent process of assimilation that immigrant groups have often experienced in the United States, a process that once affected the Irish, Italians, and Jews and now affects South Asian, Middle Eastern, Hispanic, and other immigrants from the Southern Hemisphere. The fact that fiction writers representing these communities have so consistently thematized these issues affirms the significance of Behdad's observation.

The Muslim characters in *The Girl in the Tangerine Scarf* experience a xenophobia by association; that is to say, xenophobes blame them for the actions of any and all Muslims anywhere in the world simply because they too are Muslim. Kahf's presentation of xenophobia is realistic in that conflagrations between the United States and Muslim-majority nations have consistently engendered Islamophobia, often accompanied by violence and the suspension of civil liberties. In Simmonsville, for example, the 1979 Iran hostage crisis—in which Iranian revolutionaries overthrew the American-backed shah, stormed the U.S. Embassy in Tehran, and captured fifty-two hostages—allows feelings of animosity to surface. The seizure of hostages "made America hopping mad. America was mad at Khadra personally, the Shamy family, and all the other Muslims of Indianapolis. Simmonsville residents who didn't know the Shah of Iran from Joe Schmoe yelled 'Long live the Shah!' as their Muslim neighbors got out of their cars and went into the blue house on New Harmony Drive. Vandalism of the Dawah Center with soap and white spray paint was something the police couldn't seem to stop; they only came and took pictures every time it happened" (119). This harassment of the Shamy family and its peers relies on the assumption that all Muslims share a singular belief and political outlook, an assumption that Kahf's independent-minded Muslim characters clearly disprove.

In the novel, racism does not exist simply against Muslims by whites. The Muslims are multiethnic, and these multiple ethnic groups are not themselves in complete unity. In particular, Kahf illuminates Arab and South Asian Muslims' racism toward American-born black Muslims. This issue is not often discussed in public forums, so Kahf's thematic placement of it in *The Girl in the Tangerine* scarf is a courageous adherence to realism despite the fact that it casts some

Muslims in a negative light. This racism toward African Americans does not much resemble traditional forms of American racism. There is no formal or de facto segregation, no use of racial epithets, and no theories of biological inferiority. In fact, as devout Muslims the Shamys and other immigrants believe strongly in the fundamental equality of all humans and reject any notions that one group is superior in the eyes of God.

Their racism is much more implicit than the forms of American racism that led to the systematic marginalization of African Americans in the past and that continue to foster various inequalities in the present. The narrator explains, "This was the Dawah Center line: No racism in Islam. Meaning, none is allowed; a commendable ideal. But it was also a smokescreen of denial that retarded any real attempt to deal with the prejudices that existed among Muslims" (137). As is often the case with racism, theirs is suppressed, arising only when a potential conflict requires it to surface. Wajdy and Ebtihaj consider themselves enlightened, but that self-image does not prevent them from sometimes expressing racist attitudes. These attitudes arise when Eyad approaches them about proposing to Maha Abdul-Kader, a Sudanese Muslim American whose upper-class family is involved with the Dawah Center and whose parents Wajdy and Ebtihaj consider friends. After Eyad shares his plans, "his father stopped deboning the chicken, mid-breast, and blurted, 'But for heaven's sake, she's black as coal!'" (139).

The comment represents a suppressed reality for the Shamys: "As soon as he'd said it, Wajdy looked queasy, and seemed almost taken aback that such a thing had come out of his own mouth." For his part, "Eyad seemed dazed, even paralyzed. The gulf between what they'd taught him and what was happening— and his not wanting to face that gulf even in light of what his father had just said—was overwhelming" (139). The scene, which intrepidly confronts an issue in the Muslim and Arab American communities that is often suppressed much in the same way that the Shamys suppress it, actually involves more than the simple unearthing of implicitly bigoted attitudes. It also digs up class and status issues as well.

In making his decision to propose to Maha, skin color is not important to Eyad. He imagines that his parents will care more about his spouse's ability to pass along the Arabic language to the children, a task for which Maha is eminently qualified. His main concern, in fact, is that Maha's parents will reject him because of his modest economic background. Wajdy's reaction, then, is an ironic turn of events: Eyad's insecurity about his own worthiness, based on a factor over which he has no control, ends up irrelevant when Maha becomes subject to a judgment about her worthiness over which she has no control. The scene illuminates that for Eyad's parents skin color is more important than wealth because otherwise they would likely be thrilled that their son wants to marry an Arab Muslim whose father is a well-known physician. For them, the reality of Maha's class standing is subordinate to her racial status, based solely on her appearance. Her blackness therefore signifies to the Shamys an unavoidable marker of inferiority that not even religious devotion, cultural affinity, or economic well-being can make up for.

Khadra and Eyad are not the only ones aware of tacit racism in their community. At the end of the novel, when the adult Khadra, having divorced a Kuwaiti man her parents accepted, enters into a relationship with Hakim, he reveals to her that he had a crush on her in their youth but never approached her parents about it: "'All that Muslim-on-Muslim racism,' he acknowledges. She appreciates that he is too kind to say, 'Your racist parents'" (440).

Khadra and Hakim's budding relationship is only one example of boundary crossing. The fact that their coming together is the note on which the novel ends underscores its thematic importance. *The Girl in the Tangerine Scarf* uses an ecumenical structure. Kahf not only represents Islam in America as a complex presence, humanizing its various adherents (including the apostate), but also favorably portrays people of other faiths. She does so without simplifying the many pratfalls of religious observance and carefully avoids reducing people of faith to followers without agency. The most fully realized instance of boundary crossing also occurs near the end of the novel, when Khadra's youngest brother, Jihad, confesses to her that he is in love with Sariah Whitcomb, a childhood friend who belongs to a devout Latter-Day Saint (Mormon) family.

Although it might seem that a practicing Muslim family and a practicing Mormon family would be firmly against any interreligious marriage, Jihad intends to use that devoutness to his advantage: "I didn't *ever* think I'd marry someone outside our religion. Neither did she—she told me. She grew up real religious. Actually, we first bonded over that—how strict our *parental units* are and stuff" (431). Jihad's relationship with Sariah is not merely happenstance, though; it has been rendered possible by the choices Jihad has made during his life. He is in a band with Sariah's brother, cheekily called the Clash of Civilizations, an ironic moniker intended to highlight the theory's silliness. Sariah's parents have a good relationship with Wajdy and Ebtihaj, based on their mutual respect of one another's religious values, though each family feels that the other subscribes to the incorrect religion. The main point conveyed by the novel is that theology can differ, but the practice of religion can be remarkably similar. To that end, Jihad and Khadra speculate about the religious inclinations of mixed Muslim and Mormon children:

> "They'll be Mor-lims."
> "Mus-mons?" (432)

Kahf brings seemingly disparate traditions together through the blending of language. Whatever Jihad and Sariah's children will call themselves or however they will choose to worship, the operative ethic is that choice exists, and Jihad and Sariah are able to come together in the first place. Jihad's ability to extend his ethos comes from a view of Islam that, according to Kahf, is often suppressed or overlooked in discourses about this religion in the West. "Most women who are Muslim," she has noted, "hear [an] egalitarian voice in Islam. But most outsiders just hear the hierarchical."[3]

Islam is not singular, however, a point that Kahf emphasizes throughout *The Girl in the Tangerine Scarf*. One of the novel's main themes, in fact, is the sometimes hostile dialectic between conservative and moderate Islam. The labels *conservative* and *moderate* do not really describe much of substance and should therefore be viewed as convenient but incomplete descriptors. They come out of a rigid view of Islam that is judgmental: whereas moderate Islam, with forms of practice considered amenable to Western politics, is supposedly populated by good Muslims, conservative or political Islam, with forms of practice considered detrimental to Western politics, is supposedly populated by bad Muslims. Kahf does not maintain this binary. The notions of moderate and conservative in *The Girl in the Tangerine Scarf* refer mainly to one's level of devotion, not only to Allah, but also to the normative set of practices developed by religious Muslims in the United States.

Having offered this disclaimer, I can focus on Kahf's exploration of religious devotion through the use of the tangerine scarf as a metonym. Khadra goes through various stages of devotion in the novel, which renders her symbolic in addition to realistic. These stages range from the ultrareligious to the disaffected.

Her level of devotion can often be detected by what she wears: during what she calls her "revolutionary" phase, which coincides with the Iranian hostage crisis in 1979, she covers herself in black clothing; later, during her "break" from devoutness, she does not wear a scarf or any sort of head covering at all. The moment of philosophical and moral closure arrives for her upon a journey to Syria, where she spends time with her grandmother and a mythical poet who is physically dead but spiritually alive. As Khadra settles into her airline seat upon her departure from Syria, she is able to integrate the many components of her ethnic and religious identity, an achievement articulated through the scarf:

> On the plane, she pulled the tangerine silk out of her handbag. Pulled and pulled, and drew the head-covering out longer and longer in her hands like like [sic] an endless handkerchief from a magician's pocket. Before landing in Chicago, she draped the depatta so it hung from the crown of her head. Not tightly, the way Ebtihaj wore it. Loosely, so it moved and slipped about her face and touched her cheek, like the hand of a lover. She wanted them to know at Customs, at the reentry checkpoint, she wanted them to know at O'Hare, that she was coming in under one of the many signs of the heritage. (313)

This Damascene style of dress represents Khadra's ability to find comfort in her many identities, the scarf's looseness symbolic of her desire to be dynamic and adaptive. Khadra does not necessarily exemplify a multivalent Islam in America through her progression, but she allows readers to understand the realities of a multivalent Islam in America.

Khadra's adventures in various forms of acculturation lead her to other Islamic engagements that are instructive for readers. In particular, Kahf explores gender issues among Muslim Americans through Khadra, although other characters participate in important ways in those explorations. Khadra engages in an ongoing debate about the scarf with her more secular friends, for example. Seemi, who is adamantly uncovered, often tries to convince Khadra to lose the scarf, something Khadra refuses to do. After the events of September 11, 2001, when a woman's head scarf was the most reliable indicator of Muslim faith, Seemi implores, "Take the damn thing off; it's not worth risking your life for" (424). Those events, however, have only brought Khadra closer to her spirituality: "Seemi didn't get it. When you're in danger, you don't strip off your armor. . . . It was the outer sign of an inner quality she wants to be reminded of, more often than she could manage to remind herself without it" (424–25). The description of the scarf as armor presents the reader with a complex metaphor. It indicates that the scarf is a form of protection in a world that can be hostile, but also that it shields whoever wears it from straying away from the values that sustain her.

Other important gender issues in *The Girl in the Tangerine Scarf* include divorce and abortion, which Khadra undertakes simultaneously. After she marries Juma al-Tashkenti, a Kuwaiti who is described as a "good" and "practicing" Muslim, the seemingly idyllic relationship begins to decline, a subtle reality that becomes evident when Khadra refuses to abandon her bicycle. When she hops on her bike to visit the grocery store, Juma "looked puzzled. She was an Arab girl, familiar with Arab customs. He hadn't expected her to be doing things that embarrassed him" (227). After constant arguing about the bike, Juma finally "pulled rank. 'I forbid you,' he said, laying his hand on the bike seat. 'As your husband, I forbid you'" (230). This demand, to which Khadra reluctantly submits, foregrounds their inevitable separation, before which she concludes, "I don't think I can stay with Juma without changing who I am. Who I essentially deep-down am" (243). Khadra learns soon after this exchange over the bicycle that she is pregnant.

With these scenes, Kahf endeavors to undermine readers' expectations about Islam vis-à-vis divorce and abortion. Based on Islamic law, Khadra is able to divorce Juma without losing all of her assets, and she subsequently undergoes an abortion that her disapproving parents must ultimately accept. Here the multifaceted qualities of Islam become conspicuous. One version of Islamic devotion allows Khadra's husband, brother, and parents to maintain customs and beliefs that are essentially repressive. Another version, which is not necessarily discrete, allows Khadra to pursue actions that for her are liberatory. Kahf thus presents readers with a fictive reflection on Islam that takes into account its many and sometimes conflicting uses and manifestations. Rather than existing as a social prison for women, which political discourse in the United States commonly asserts, Islam as presented in *The Girl in the Tangerine Scarf* actually endows women with progressive options for the use of their bodies that often are withheld from religious Christian women.

Another interesting point Kahf presents through Khadra and Juma's relationship is the inadequacy of perceived cultural similarities as a basis for relationships. In other words, Kahf appears to put forth the belief that sharing culture is not enough to make a relationship work; other things, such as patience and open-mindedness, are required. In addition, the very idea of a cultural profile is troublesome because it ignores substantial differences within apparently singular communities: both Khadra and Juma are Arab Muslims, but they adhere to markedly different versions of personal behavior and religious devotion. Khadra actually has much more in common with people her parents would not want her to marry. Part of the reason that she can walk away from a Muslim cultural tradition is ironically that she is Muslim. Islam, it becomes clear in *The Girl in the Tangerine Scarf*, allows her to be who she feels she is at her most fundamental.

Other representations of Islam as a positive social and personal force include its emphasis on service to humanity and its ability to engender familial closeness. These representations, coupled with Kahf's willingness to show Muslims in a negative light, produce a distinct antidogmatic sensibility throughout the novel, one exemplified by Khadra's many disagreements with friends and family. With her adamantly secular friend (and short-lived lover) Chrif, for instance, Khadra often finds herself frustrated by what she perceives as his intransigence, which to her ironically resembles the sort of narrowness she encounters among devout Muslims. After one such argument, "Khadra sighed. She just wanted to make him admit that being Muslim wasn't such a straitjacket. It was the same argument she had with her mother. She didn't expect Chrif to be arguing for the same thing as her mother, that Islam was rigid and homogenous. It's like, they *both* wanted Islam to be this monolith, only for her mother it was good, for him bad. She knew it wasn't that simple" (344). Although Kahf writes in a plainspoken style, one that conveys a narrative simplicity, she presents myriad conflicts and concerns that are far from simple.

The Girl in the Tangerine Scarf often reads like a social document embedded in the genre of fiction. Characters usually embody specific political outlooks or ethical commitments. In this way, the characters are both realistic and allegorical. This dual burden is exemplified by Zuhura, who exists mostly as a remembered character. As a realistic character, Zuhura demonstrates integrity, beauty, strength, and positive ambition. Her effect as a symbolic character is even greater, however. Khadra characterizes Zuhura's rape and murder as "a thing everybody knew. A sign for all to consider" (428). By releasing all of her suppressed mourning for Zuhura, Khadra highlights Zuhura's symbolic importance because Zuhura's death has become indivisible from Khadra's own growth. Her death, in other words, has entered into the everyday reality of everybody's lives. Only when Khadra finally confronts and accepts the horror of Zuhura's death and the meaning of Zuhura's life is she able to move forward with a sense of wholeness comprising her numerous identities.

In a sense, *The Girl in the Tangerine Scarf* acts as a primer on Islam in America, replete with an exploration of different Muslim ethnicities, in particular African and Arab American. Although it is important for literary critics to situate social themes within their aesthetic settings, *The Girl in the Tangerine Scarf* lends itself to a sociopolitical reading because of its obvious activist dimensions. Much of the novel's philosophical and poetic apparatus relies on Khadra, whose numerous transformations symbolize a multiplicity of Arab and Muslim worldviews. Kahf complicates what it means to have "Arab" or "Islamic" customs and cultures. She shows these communities to be complex entities that exist beyond caricature.

One of the novel's noteworthy features is Kahf's refusal to avoid issues that are controversial within Arab and Muslim American communities, but that are generally unknown by those who do not belong to or interact with these groups. Popularly known as "airing dirty laundry," a phrase that has negative connotations, this refusal generates debate in ethnic, religious, and political communities around the world. Kahf airs dirty laundry, which is another way of saying she is an honest writer, a true advocate of her craft and her community. She illuminates Arab and Muslim Americans in their totality, including the negative, which ultimately makes them more human and thus more likeable. Perhaps this thoroughness is the most notable aspect of *The Girl in the Tangerine Scarf*: the fact that Kahf shows people to be a repository of so many problems and yet never allows readers to lose their faith in humankind.

4

Sex, Violence, and Storytelling

Rabih Alameddine

BASED ON A COMBINATION OF critical and commercial success, Rabih Alameddine, of Lebanese Druze background, is the preeminent Arab American novelist today. (The Druze are a religious minority in Lebanon, Syria, and Palestine.) His three novels—*Koolaids: The Art of War, I, the Divine: A Novel in First Chapters,* and *The Hakawati*—are remarkably imaginative (as is his collection of short stories, *The Perv*). Although Alameddine's writing focuses on a cluster of themes—the Lebanese Civil War, sexuality/homosexuality, family relations, racism, myths, and stories—each of his novels stands alone aesthetically. His most recent novel, *The Hakawati,* draws from some of the structures he employed in *Koolaids* and *I, the Divine,* but on the whole it is his magnum opus, a unique blend of traditional storytelling, mythology, religious narrative, and modern novel. *Koolaids* is a nonlinear pastiche. *I, the Divine* is a complete novel, but it never technically moves beyond the first chapter. Alameddine's work is difficult to explicate because it does not conform to any traditional categories. This difficulty makes it rewarding to critique, however. Let us look at his three novels in chronological order.

Koolaids

I have taught *Koolaids* to undergraduates on numerous occasions. The first time I taught it, I was quite nervous given the novel's graphic sexual imagery and its ridicule of sacred cows such as religion and patriotism, not to mention its unorthodox structure. I was pleasantly surprised that my students loved the novel, despite the fact that many of them had difficulty comprehending its story line. The main reason they were able to enjoy *Koolaids* is that Alameddine succeeds in emphasizing humor and irreverence in the story. My student readers responded favorably to this humor and irreverence.

I will share with you the advice that I always offer to others before they begin reading *Koolaids*. Whether you are a professional writer, a casual reader, or a student who has been assigned the novel, I hope that the advice will prove useful: just read. That is to say, do not spend all of your time figuring out who is narrating, determining where every scene takes place, and identifying every minor celebrity or religious figure. These elements, although certainly important, are nearly impossible to decipher completely. *Koolaids* is not a normal novel, so it must be read abnormally. Whereas the logistical details of a narrative are generally integral to both the enjoyment and comprehension of a novel, this is not necessarily the case with *Koolaids*. Part of its appeal is its decentralized narrative, one that allows readers to understand the flow and progress of the story differently than they usually would. This style is possible in part because Alameddine is telling numerous stories at once. They manage to come together into something coherent, albeit not in a traditional sense, when the reader does not intently focus on mechanics and instead focuses on the simple act of reading.

Koolaids has two main protagonists, Samir Bashar and Mohammad (no last name mentioned), both artists and both gay Lebanese immigrants to San Francisco. They often become intertwined in the narrative, along with Makram and a host of non–Lebanese American characters, in particular Ben and Kurt. The point of view is usually developed through the male characters, but Alameddine also employs women narrators: Joumana Bashar, Samir's sister; Samia Marchi, who has a deadly tryst with a Christian militia leader; Laura, Kurt's sister; and Marwa, Mohammad's sister. Samir and Mohammad encounter one another at one point, but for the most part each has a separate story wherein they both exist in the same broad social circle, that of gay, educated artists in the Bay Area. Mohammad is a Muslim, Samir a Druze, and Makram a Christian. Each represents a different sectarian group, although none of them maintains his sectarian position to the point of its becoming a primary identity.

Koolaids is a pastiche that mixes not only story lines and temporal sequences, but also styles and genres. Alameddine reproduces news stories, proffers dialogue in a playwriting format, interrupts sequences with sarcastic commentaries, and includes conversations among dead (and living) celebrities and deities. This combination of reportage and literary montage renders *Koolaids* unique in the modern Arab American canon and one of the more original works of American fiction more generally. The style is *postmodern,* a term that denotes many things at once. There is postmodern theology, theory, art, and architecture. In literature, *postmodernism,* although not a singular term, describes a style that is highly suspicious of static meaning and of tidy story lines and resolutions. Postmodern novels, then, tend to utilize pastiche and sometimes border on (or enter into) the surreal in terms of their plots, philosophies, and dialogues. Think of postmodern literature as what a decentralized worldview looks like when somebody manages to apply it to paper.

The fact that *Koolaids* uses postmodern techniques does not mean that it is devoid of moral or political substance. Alameddine explores two primary moral and political themes: the AIDS epidemic and the Lebanese Civil War, from which the pun in the subtitle is drawn. He juxtaposes the two phenomena, showing both of them to be without ready logic and presenting one of the novel's central ironies: because of AIDS, sex, which humans participate in as a life-bearing act, has become a harbinger of death. In the inverse, war inevitably produces death, but it is always justified as a necessary affirmation of life. In *Koolaids,* Mohammad explores this juxtaposition in a book he speaks of writing but never actually writes: "When I first started seeing my friends die, I wanted to write a book where all the characters died in the beginning, say in the first twenty-five pages or so. I never went beyond the incipit, which I thought was a damn good one. *Death comes in many shapes and sizes, but it always comes.* I thought it was great. I wanted to make sure death and sex were associated."[1] In many ways, *Koolaids* represents the book that Mohammad never wrote. Alameddine certainly makes sure that death and sex are associated, a move that highlights the politics of intercourse and the basic violence of being human. Or, to be more blatant, sex is never a neutral act—it is always in some way political. And being human means that violence is possible, always just around the corner. *Koolaids* focuses on these realities.

Alameddine also explores the heterogeneity of Lebanese identity; in other words, the fact that Lebanon is such a confluence of racial, ethnic, religious, and cultural admixtures means that the quest for a unified "Lebanese" identity will be incomplete or will conflict with another version of national identity. Moreover, segments in Lebanon consider it to be a fundamentally Western culture, whereas others view it as an integral part of the Arab and Muslim worlds. Like the *chabab* of Etel Adnan's *Sitt Marie Rose,* one of the narrators of *Koolaids* observes, "We all had what some would call a European complex. We wanted so hard to be European" (28). Some Lebanese, the narrator explains, cannot even speak Arabic fluently, preferring French and preferring to commiserate only with those they perceive as likeminded. We learn later that a history book that one of the narrators—either Samir or Mohammad—studied as a schoolboy included only Christian villages, the obvious message being that the Christian community represents the real Lebanon. *Koolaids,* in both structure and theme, challenges this sort of narrow-mindedness, which can be described as ethnonationalism (a form of organizing around perceived similarities of culture, religion, or ethnicity). Alameddine decentralizes what it means to be Lebanese rather than upholding a particular version of it.

In fact, the very notion of ethnic or cultural boundaries seems anathema to Alameddine. The novel includes visible social critiques, however. Alameddine, for example, examines stereotypes about Arabs in the United States as well as stereotypes that Lebanese have about Americans. At one point, the narrator explains, "[Americans] think we are all crazy, maybe even degenerate. The only way they make our suffering palatable is by envisioning us as less than human" (54). And one sector of the Maronite community believes that the Lebanese are descended from the ancient Phoenicians, a way to anchor themselves in an imagined past that renders them properly indigenous and a way to distinguish themselves from other sectarian communities that do not have the same claim to Lebanon. A letter from somebody in the novel named Roger Dabbas, which may be a reproduction of an actual essay or correspondence, sums up this belief: "In summation, Maronites are NOT Arabs, never were, never will be. We are Syrio-Aramaic. We are Phoenicians. We need to be proud of our heritage and revive it. We need to throw away the Arab shackles that everybody tries to bind us with. We are not Arabs. We are Lebanese. Lebanon is the homeland of Christians. We shall refuse to live under occupation. We will always be Christian, always Lebanese" (59). Dabbas's letter, like all expressions of ethnonationalism, is replete with dubious history, but representing history accurately is not its point. Its point is to invoke an imagined past in order to construct a modern political identity (even if that identity masquerades as purely cultural). In this way, his letter is more like a manifesto than a history lesson. It is deeply invested in the sectarian strife that it claims to rise above. Throughout

Koolaids, Alameddine treats these episodes of ethnonationalism as being in themselves violent in addition to illustrating the physical violence they produce. Just as he does not limit the concepts of "Lebanese" and "Lebanon" to singular, static items, he does not confine violence to the realm of physical engagement. He shows it also to be discursive (a product of discourses).

Violent discourse exists throughout the novel—in scenes in which gay men with AIDS are blamed for the decline of humanity and said to be beyond sympathy; in the various strands of ethnonationalism that motivate actors in the Lebanese Civil War; and in the seemingly lighthearted banter among the Lebanese and American characters, which sometimes reveals insensitivity bordering on racism. One advantage to *Koolaids*'s ambiguous narration is the ability it has to remove authority from a single individual or an ethnic collective. Alameddine cleverly deploys a structure appropriate to his novel's philosophical irreverence. A noteworthy result of his choice is that *Koolaids* achieves the status of a highly complex story: it juxtaposes two seemingly disparate phenomena but does not make them binaristic. Alameddine's juxtaposition of AIDS and the Lebanese Civil War is unorthodox but appropriate: it conceptualizes AIDS as a form of violence and war as a form of disease, a move away from traditional definitions. He thus asks readers to think differently about the categories they normally use to make sense of things.

The category of "Arab," for example, brings to mind a set of images for many Americans, some of them contradictory: brutish, misogynistic, untrustworthy, sexually voracious, greedy. All categories retain their meaning based on a set of static images and assumptions. In *Koolaids,* Alameddine complicates the categories surrounding both Arabs and Americans. He not only presents various cultures of homosexuality but couches many of them within the broader framework of Arab culture rather than making the two mutually exclusive. The same is true of secularism, intellectualism, and women's rights. The things that are often set apart from notions of Arab culture, then, play a direct role in decentralizing and redefining that culture in *Koolaids.*

The episodes of violence and death that pervade *Koolaids* ultimately create a form of meaning that is ambivalent but necessary for the characters to survive. As Mohammad points out in a passage he falsely attributes to the Scottish writer Muriel Sparks, "If I had my life over again, I would form the habit of nightly composing myself to thoughts of death. I would practice the remembrance of death.

There is no other practice which so intensifies life. Death, when it approaches, ought not to take one by surprise. It should be part of the full expectancy of life. Without an ever-present sense of death, life is insipid. You might as well live on the whites of eggs. You might as well drink Kool-Aid" (99). It is difficult to tell whether this passage is sincere or sarcastic. I tend to view it as cheeky, a viewpoint that is indeed serious but supplemented by a playful sense of irony, something that can be said of *Koolaids* in total. After all, what better metaphor is there to describe the novel's philosophy than a drink that is colorful enough to promise something exciting but that is actually a saccharine illusion?

I, the Divine

I, the Divine, like *Koolaids,* is a remarkably imaginative novel. "A novel in first chapters," it in fact never moves into a chapter 2. However, the subtitle is slightly misleading; some of the first chapters are actually introductions. In any case, the novel is not a singular narrative. It is a collection of the protagonist's failed attempts to complete a memoir and a novel. In the failed attempts, though, a coherent story comes through, one that informs the reader as much about the act of writing as it does about the lives of the novel's characters.

I, *the Divine* mixes genres, something of a signature for Alameddine. Although the book in total is technically fiction, some of its constituent parts are more difficult to label. The protagonist, Sarah Nour El-Din, who is ostensibly named after the transcendent French actress Sarah Bernhardt, wants to be a writer but never manages to complete a project. She at first attempts a memoir, then a novel (which is suspiciously autobiographical). At one point, she uses the epistolary form (a novel told through letter correspondence). One of the sections, "The Fall," is not identified as a memoir or a novel, and certain subsections are not listed as either a first chapter or an introduction. There is enough structural ambiguity in I, *the Divine* to preclude it from a tidy characterization. Each genre reveals something different about the extensive history that Sarah attempts to present. The use of only first chapters likewise enables Alameddine to create a complex story. In retelling the same stories in different chapters, Sarah actually reveals much more than a linear structure would allow. Such episodic shifts are also philosophically important: they speak to the tenuousness of storytelling as a foolproof mode of communication by highlighting the inevitable multiplicity that exists in the act of remembering something and then speaking about it. Or, to put it more simply, there are many sides to the same story. Sarah proves this point repeatedly in *I, the Divine*. Alameddine thrives on its possibilities.

Part of Sarah's difficulty in producing a sustained narrative is her own heterogeneous background, which she views as being fragmented. Born to a Lebanese father and a white American mother, she spent her childhood in Lebanon but immigrated to the United States and as an adult is loath to return to the Middle East. She reminisces about the travails of her dual identity: "I hated Umm Kalthoum [a famous Egyptian singer]. I wanted to identify only with my American half. I wanted to be special. I could not envision how to be Lebanese and keep any sense of individuality."[2] In another incarnation of the same theme, she writes, "I have been blessed with many curses in my life, not the least of which was being born half Lebanese and half American" (229). These passages underscore the verbal panache that reflects Sarah's ambivalence. In the first passage, she reproduces two separate binaries: one that says a cultural identity can be parsed into percentages in the same way that biological origin can and another that reinforces the conception of the United States as individualistic and Lebanon as communal. In the second passage, she appears to reproduce the same lament, but in fact she complicates the binaries by employing an oxymoron—"blessed with many curses"—that makes it difficult to figure out whether her Lebanese or American half is the burden. If it is neither, then Sarah has at least momentarily integrated the two identities.

Later in her life, Sarah comes to understand that one's identity is not so easily parsed into (artificial) categories. "Only recently," she observes, "have I begun to realize that like my city, my American patina covers an Arab soul" (229). She ultimately realizes, in a sentiment that reveals one of the novel's central themes, that compartmentalizing her identity is a losing proposition: "Throughout my life, these contradictory parts battled endlessly, clashed, never coming to a satisfactory conclusion. I shuffled ad nauseam between the need to assert my individuality and the need to belong to my clan, being terrified of loneliness and terrorized of losing myself in relationships" (229). Sarah's sense of self is tied into ways of identifying that are unsustainable because they create expectations that are never fully matched by experience. The clashes arose because they were the only logical outcome to her separation of individuality and clan. Her recognition of this fact is one of the climactic moments in her development as a character.

Sarah has difficulty moving beyond a first chapter because the story she attempts to tell is not cohesive. Many of her perceptions about her past and her family get disrupted by other characters' memories; the novel's multiple perspectivism allows these competing visions to be accommodated. For instance, she fondly remembers her grandfather Hammoud, who for her symbolizes a romanticized past, as a humorous (sometimes mischievous) and affectionate person. She eventually learns, however, that, according to her sister Amal, "he was a misogynist. He hated all us girls. He thought all women were whores. He beat Grandmother up on a regular basis. You were just too young to remember" (287). It turns out that Hammoud showered affection on the young Sarah simply because she was unwittingly aiding his plan to get her mother, Janet, back to the United States. Amal also reveals to Sarah that their grandfather filled her head with stories about an "apotheosized" Sarah Bernhardt because he did not like the fact that she was actually named after a female Druze hero.

These revelations, which happen at the end of the novel, force Sarah to reassess her past and her various relationships with others, in particular the one with her aloof mother, whose disillusionment becomes more understandable. Here Alameddine comments on the murky nature of memory and the inability to understand the past comprehensively without competing narratives. The structure of *I, the Divine* performs this theme by telling a complete story in seemingly unconnected fragments. At times, though, certain situations are repeated through different moods or points of view. Sarah recounts her adolescent discovery of sexuality and her first physical relationship (with Fadi) in separate first chapters, which allows readers to see a more complete portrayal of a singular moment in her past. As the novel progresses, Sarah manages to grow in age despite the fact that the book she is writing never evolves past a first chapter. As the literary critic Waïl S. Hassan notes, "For Sarah, these narrative genres, with their ideological assumptions about order and final resolution, cannot possibly contain her experience."[3] Readers see her from thirteen years old to middle age.

As is his custom, Alameddine explores a range of social issues, in particular sexuality and gender. For *I, the Divine*, he even uses a female narrator and tells the story from her perspective. Although in the history of fiction writing it is not unheard of for a writer of one gender to narrate through a character of a different gender, when it happens, it is noteworthy because it automatically raises questions about the author's decision making and whether the attempted transcending of imagined boundaries (such as race, class, or gender) has been done successfully. I am of the opinion that skilled writers not only can transcend imagined boundaries but *should* transcend them when appropriate. Such a choice makes the act of reading infinitely more interesting.

Sarah's best friend, Dina Ballout, to whom her memoir *I, the Divine* is devoted, is an open lesbian whose sexuality sometimes comes into conflict with the expectations of both Lebanese and American society. Through this character, Alameddine complicates the popular notion that whereas Americans are inherently open-minded, Arabs are stubbornly homophobic. Sarah's younger half-brother, Ramzi, is likewise homosexual and is portrayed by Sarah as having always been fastidious: "Ever since he was a boy, Ramzi had been meticulous. Whenever we went to the beach, he wore a tight Speedo and his penis always pointed upward. To this day, whenever I see him in a bathing suit, his penis is never pointing left or right, always up" (123). This description, simultaneously humorous and revelatory, places emphasis on Ramzi's sexual organ as a way of illuminating his personality, which suggests that sexuality and identity are indivisible. Alameddine moves beyond nationality and ethnicity in his appraisal of human relationships.

As he does in *Koolaids,* he also ridicules the rigidity of religious discourse, one of the main foundations of sectarianism. The young Sarah's grandfather, for instance, gives her an interesting lesson on Christianity: "Remember, Jesus is only for children and people who never get smart" (280). Hammoud does not spare Muslims his comic wrath, explaining to Sarah that the Muslim pilgrimage (the hajj) consists of "the silly Muslims who go to Mecca and walk in white dresses" (280). Although on the surface it may seem unnecessary to inculcate a child with such an explicit suspicion of religion, the scene performs a useful narrative and philosophical function in *I, the Divine:* it reveals a humanistic lesson about unreflective religiosity's ability to suppress creativity and independent thought, a lesson imparted through the story of Sarah Bernhardt's exclusion from a school play by "the fat guy in a dress" (the Catholic archbishop). In Hammoud's mind, divinity does not require the presence of God; it can be achieved through human pursuits. No matter her grandfather's shortcomings, this lesson is one that Sarah realizes throughout her life.

Of course, the lesson is not a panacea, nor does it prevent Sarah from encountering the difficulties inherent in conflating sexuality with identity. Her "anachronistic" father, Mustapha, is simultaneously traditional and progressive, his traditionalism focused mainly on the importance of a woman's honor, which is tied directly to her sexual choices (or merely to her reputation vis-à-vis sexual choices). A philanderer, Mustapha holds women to a decidedly more stringent standard: "'A boy's sexuality is like a plastic tablecloth,' he said. 'If a carafe of wine is spilled on it, you can easily wipe it off. A girl's sexuality, on the other hand, is like fine linen, much more valuable. If a carafe of wine is spilled on it, it will never come off. You can wash it and wash it, but it can never be the same'" (127). Mustapha's analogy conflates virginity and cleanliness; it assumes that a woman can be stained, whereas a man is fundamentally impervious to dishonor, a viewpoint that severely restricts the range of activities in which a woman can engage. Sarah subsequently considers herself a "black sheep" of her family because of her sexual relationships and divorces.

These notions of honor are pervasive in Mustapha's identity, to the point where Sarah thinks of him immediately when they find out that her older sister Lamia has been arrested and charged with serial killings. "I am ashamed to admit my first reaction was not concern for Lamia, but for my father," she confesses (126). The revelation of Lamia's crimes forms the novel's emotional and thematic climax, bringing members of the Nour El-Din (Light of Religion) family together and forcing them to confront issues that might otherwise be suppressed. All Lamia's victims were in the hospital. As Sarah explains, "She hated her job as a nurse. She thought the patients too demanding so she systematically killed those who most annoyed her while under her care" (147). Lamia managed to kill seven patients and attempted to kill two others. Her troubled psychology is linked to her absent mother, to whom she wrote unsent letters for nearly four decades. The letters reveal many of Lamia's psychological problems, especially an endemic sense of isolation and displeasure with her father and stepmother. Her broken English and rambling stream of consciousness further highlight a detachment from the moral consequences of her behavior.

In fact, Lamia may not actually be Lamia. She is a "talker," a reincarnation of a departed soul in the Druze religion. As a child, she spoke of a well-heeled life in Jabal Al-Druze (Druze Mountain) in Syria. It turns out she "had come from a rich, landowning family and had three kids of her own" (148). Although Lamia, according to Sarah, "knew the exact details of her life in Jabal Al-Druze," Sarah ultimately attributes her actions to insanity. Alameddine leaves it to the reader to sort out Lamia's competing motivations. Her symbolic importance in the novel is discernible, however. She embodies the sort of violence that can arise from detachment. She also catalyzes the other characters, indicating that a sense of community often develops in response to tragedy. Most important, Lamia is Sarah's "least favorite sister" and frequently acts as her nemesis or antagonist. In this way, she serves as Sarah's foil (a character that contrasts with the protagonist, often revealing or even reflecting important features of the protagonist's ethics and personality). Lamia appears to be aware of this role, writing, "Sarah she swallows life out of her men" (156).

Lamia ascribes a violence to Sarah's sexuality, which turns out not to be completely farfetched. In the second half of the novel, readers learn that Sarah was once detained and gang-raped, an act that for obvious reasons has produced the trauma that disallows Sarah to move beyond a first chapter. It is noteworthy that she recounts the trauma in her "fiction," presenting the scene using a third-person narrator. This shift in genre invests Sarah in the story without directly situating her in it. The terrible event becomes a seminal moment in *I, the Divine*. As Hassan notes, after Sarah recounts the gang rape, "things begin to fall into place: her chronic depression, her broken relationships, her inability to help the dying AIDS patients whom she volunteers to counsel, her restless wanderings from San Francisco to New York to Beirut and back again, and her obsession with storytelling coupled with total rejection of canonical narrative genres."[4]

Alameddine explores the political factors that contribute to the crime committed against Sarah. That crime arises from the breakdown of order that has resulted from the onset of the Lebanese Civil War. The horrible effects of war reveal themselves in Sarah's trauma and in the many acts of violence that might otherwise be considered random. Alameddine suggests philosophically that human behavior and human stories inevitably converge, so Sarah cannot tell a story about the civil war without confronting the terrible misdeed committed against her. Although *I, the Divine* first appears to be fragmented, it is actually a highly integrated and fluid story. Perhaps its fluidity is best exemplified by a seemingly inconsequential line about Sarah's friend Dina, who "showed up" in West Beirut, "crossing from East Beirut" (67). The line turns out not to be inconsequential at all. Instead, it symbolizes all the difficulties and rewards offered by the act of transcending personal and political boundaries.

The Hakawati

In Lebanon's colloquial dialect, *hakawati* means "storyteller," but it does not refer to just a conventional storyteller. A *hakawati*—an effective one, anyway—is a performer and an entertainer, sometimes a trickster, who is able to keep his audience enraptured for days on end. A proper *hakawati* has a great deal of knowledge but is also able to be spontaneously inventive. He also preserves a community's history and passes it along to future generations. He is in many ways the voice of the past in the ever-changing present. Rabih Alameddine is a fine example of a *hakawati*.

Although Alameddine is still a young writer and artist, it is difficult to imagine that *The Hakawati* will not in the future be considered his magnum opus. An epic novel whose length belies its tightness, *The Hakawati* has been billed by many critics as a modern *Arabian Nights,* the ancient Arabic tales narrated by Scheherazade. I tend to find such comparisons a bit exaggerated, even though *Arabian Nights* clearly has influenced both *The Hakawati* and the storytelling traditions from which it draws and which it represents. Comparisons to *Arabian Nights,* however, overlook the modern fictive techniques that frame *The Hakawati* and situate it in other important traditions, such as modernism and American immigrant literature. The novel does contain an epic presence, which makes it all the more difficult to categorize.

The Hakawati resembles *I, the Divine* more than it does *Koolaids,* though like the other two books it is structurally unique. In many ways, reading *The Hakawati* feels like engaging three or four novels simultaneously. In very broad terms, it contains dual (but not necessarily competing) narratives: one, the telling of stories from various Middle Eastern cultures, including religious, historical, mythological, and newfangled tales of courage, adventure, and redemption; the other a story focused on a massive, multiethnic Lebanese family whose members live in the United States and the Middle East and who frequently cross the Atlantic physically and imaginatively.

There are things that *The Hakawati* is not. It is not a meditation on cultural identities; it is not a re-creation of Arab history; and it is not an allegory of modern geopolitics. I raise this point because a small but steady critical quarter has reacted to the novel by deeming it one or all of these things. Writing in the *New*

York Times, for example, Lorraine Adams wonders, "Was the narrator's first name, Osama, an intentional reference to Osama bin Laden? After all, his last name, Al-Kharrat, means 'the fibster' in Arabic."[5] This speculation is bizarre and borders on the offensive. The name "Osama" predates bin Laden of al-Qaida fame by centuries, so not every usage of it obliquely or directly references the terrorist. Adams's speculation also devalues *The Hakawati* by reducing it to a political essence that it does not even mention, much less analyze. I raise my objection in the service of a broader point—that Arab American literature need not be reduced to its (real or imagined) sociopolitical framework because it is not always written with that framework in mind. Even when such correlations are evident, it is important to remember we are dealing with art, not with political essays. I always urge folks to read Arab American literature with aesthetics and not just sociologica in mind. Alameddine practically forces readers into this emphasis.

In terms of aesthetics, Alameddine employs a grab bag of devices, in particular foreshadowing, as when Osama muses, "When it would be my time to leave, I hoped I'd go quickly, suddenly and unexpectedly, like Uncle Jihad," shortly before Jihad's sudden death occurs.[6] Another noteworthy device is the complex use of dialogue to tell stories, wherein readers often encounter an unnamed omniscient narrator as well as remembered dialogue (stories told within a story). Alameddine uses this complex dialogue to streamline the many different strands of the novel into something cohesive, although it would be inaccurate to argue that those strands follow a logical progression. One might expect Alameddine to connect the sections dealing with the modern narrative in obvious ways to the sections dealing with the ancient narratives, but he does not make such obvious connections. Those he makes are instead well wrought and subtle. The ancient world does not necessarily mirror the modern one in *The Hakawati,* although they are profoundly linked.

The stories of the ancient world are especially rich, filled with outlandish tales of conquest and redemption that always provide a moral allegory. Readers learn about Fatima, whose symbol, an eyeball encased in a palm, is represented on charms hanging on walls throughout the Arab world and used to ward off the evil eye. We hear of the rise of the heroic Baybars, who evolves from slave to king through his courage. We are introduced to a religious mythology that conjoins Judaism, Christianity, and Islam, mainly through the twins Layl and Shams, who bring together the legend of Isaac and Ismael (Hebrew: Ishmael), fathers of the Jews and the Arabs, respectively. Not only do Layl and Shams have names that symbolize darkness and light, but their skin is colored accordingly, with the dark Layl abhorred by the emir's conniving wife. This intricate use of binaries reflects Alameddine's verbal playfulness and his devotion to a form of storytelling that opens rather than closes interpretive possibilities. At one point, Layl and Shams are separated, to the great detriment of the emir and his wife, prompting Shams's transformation "from the worshipped to the mocked" and a name change to "Majnoun" (Crazy) (478). Majnoun is eventually resurrected from an attempted suicide and reunited with his real mother, Fatima, and his twin, thus restoring balance to the world and making "his love whole" (505).

Even though the content of the ancient stories is serious, their telling is not always serious in kind. They are inflected with clever and raunchy jokes, well-placed sarcasm, and fantastical sexual escapades. Nor are the perspectives of these stories static. In one telling, for example, King Baybars is a hero. According to Osama's uncle Jihad, however, Baybars "wasn't a decent ruler. His subjects despised him, because he was a ruthless, fork-tongued megalomaniac who rose to power through treachery and murder" (440). Baybars, Uncle Jihad tells Osama, was "a marketing hero" and "the precursor to all the Arab presidents we have today" (441). Uncle Jihad explains the lesson of the story to a disappointed Osama: "You see, the hakawatis' audience is the common man who couldn't really identify with a royal, almost infallible hero, so early on the hakawatis began to introduce characters that their audience could empathize with. The tale, even during its inchoate years, was never about Baybars, but those around him. The story of the king is the story of the people, and unfortunately, to this day, no king has learned that lesson" (441). This lesson has two broad themes: that a good story is always allegorical and that the allegory should be focused somehow on the popular will of the community from which it arises. According to Uncle Jihad, stories like the one about Baybars come to symbolize the disjunction between centers of power and the people who sustain but are excluded from them.

I noted earlier that *The Hakawati* resembles *I, the Divine* more than it does *Koolaids*. This opinion is based on the novel's modern narrative, which is similar (though far from identical) to the narrative of *I, the Divine* in that both explore the saga of an extended Lebanese family on two continents, and both are oriented around a protagonist who is dealing with family strife and the death of a family patriarch. In *The Hakawati*, two deaths propel the narrative by bringing conflicts to a head and drawing families together: Uncle Jihad's sudden, unexpected collapse and later the slow disintegration through terminal illness of Farid, Osama's father and Jihad's brother, business partner, and best friend. As the youngest among his siblings, Jihad, a witty and intelligent character who serves as something of a confidant and father figure to Osama, bridges the familial generations represented in the novel. He also acts as one of its seminal *hakawati*s.

Jihad functions as a catalyst in other ways. It is to Jihad, not to Farid, that Osama's mother, Layla, was initially attracted. Jihad is gay, however, a fact that Alameddine suggests but never states explicitly. Jihad helps to facilitate the courtship of Farid and Layla; after their marriage, Jihad is Layla's primary confidant. Jihad and Osama likewise have a tight relationship, and Jihad tells Osama stories throughout Osama's childhood, supplementing the influence of Osama's paternal grandfather, who taught him about the tradition of the *hakawati*s. Osama's grandfather and his son Jihad do not share many other interests and opinions, though. The grandfather is still loyal to the bey, an anachronistic communal patriarch whom Alameddine shows to be pompous and greedy. Jihad and Farid despise the bey and the hierarchy he represents, which induces fealty and reinforces undemocratic social systems. Jihad represents a transition from the bey's social system to one that is less paternalistic and more critical of tradition. This transition helps the social ethos inscribed in the novel to evolve.

Despite the many social and philosophical changes that occur in the novel, Osama's grandfather manages to impart universal advice. At one point, he tells Osama, "No matter how good a story is, there is more at stake in the telling" (96). This maxim is crucial to *The Hakawati*'s purpose and structure. First, it cleverly places the onus of quality on Alameddine as the person who presents a story in the form of a novel to the reader. Although his stories are good (a matter of opinion, admittedly), he is still responsible for presenting them with skill and élan. The maxim is philosophically more complex. It intimates that truth or believability in a story is actually secondary to the listener's ability, through a good telling, to imagine truth or believability. It further intimates that a story is not composed simply of its content, but also of its performance. Story in this framework becomes an interactive art that requires the participation of the audience, which can happen only through the strength of the tale's telling. Osama's grandfather highlights the sensual qualities of the art.

Alameddine's storytelling in *The Hakawati* is certainly notable—interesting enough, in any case, to disrupt simplistic ideologies about culture, sexuality, and history. This function is perhaps the novel's most noteworthy feature and produces its most relevant irony: that the story not only disrupts ideologies and takes them apart, but also produces a bond that draws people together. After his father's death, Osama realizes, "My father and I may have shared numerous experiences, but, as I was constantly finding out, we rarely shared their stories; we didn't know how to listen to one another" (450). This inability to listen produces chronic problems not only interpersonally, but also geopolitically. As such, *The Hakawati* is filled with verbal and military violence borne of difference. Osama and Farid's relationship is therefore a microcosm of the larger story in which it is framed.

The most obvious larger conflict is the Lebanese Civil War, which, as in Alameddine's other work, underlines much of the action even if it is not always front and center. Ancient wars also abound in the novel. It might appear that the ancient wars are more easily resolved than the modern Lebanese Civil War, but upon closer inspection this is not the case. Alameddine does not separate the various epochs of *The Hakawati* into distinct categories. Where an ancient story might end with a heroic and magical vanquishing of evil, it nevertheless offers a moral that has still not been understood by the time the modern civil war rages. Take the character of Elie, for example. An Orthodox Christian, Elie seems fated for a militia early in his life. At age thirteen, he tells a confused seven-year-old Osama that "we" are going to humiliate the Israelis at the onset of the 1967 War. (The 1967 War is also referred to as the Six-Day War, in which Israel defeated Egypt, Syria, and Jordan, capturing and occupying the Palestinian West Bank and Gaza Strip, the Egyptian Sinai Peninsula, and the Syrian Golan Heights. But propaganda in the Arab world repeatedly proclaimed victory despite the fact that the Israelis had destroyed the Egyptian air force before it even had an opportunity to attack.) Osama asks Elie who "we" refers to:

> "We," Elie said dismissively. "We, the Arabs."
> "Of course we are. Don't you know anything?"
> "I thought we're Lebanese."
> "We're that, too," Elie said. "The Lebanese haven't started fighting yet, but we will. The Israelis didn't attack us, but we're not going to wait. We'll crush them." (147)

Elie's naïveté is not the most interesting aspect of this exchange. After all, a thir-teen-year-old is bound to believe the false promises made by political leaders.

The most interesting aspect of the exchange is Elie's conceptualization of the Lebanese as "Arab" despite the fact that many Lebanese, as illustrated by Osama's comment, do not agree. It is Elie's desire to belong to a community whose unity has been invented that underlies his attraction to armed struggle. He is influ-enced by slogans devoid of any real substance. He is also sexually aggressive, sleeping with the teenage Mariella Farouk and later impregnating Osama's sister, Lina. Alameddine again connects a character's sexual appetite to his militaristic tendencies. The desire for power and destruction that propels ancient characters such as King Cade, Azkoul, and the emir are evident in the character of Elie, who proves to be weak at heart, leaving Lina immediately at the close of their shotgun wedding. The Al-Kharrat family, including Lina, considers Elie to be stupid, a feeling that in perhaps the novel's best example of understated comedy is sub-stantiated by one of Elie's beliefs: "France is our secret weapon" (147).

The entire foundation of sectarianism—the idea that one group is biologically and culturally unified and deserving of special privileges—is inherently faulty, and that's why sectarianism never accomplishes anything other than unresolved violence. If we contrast Elie with the family he marries into, we can get a better sense of what reality looks like distinctive of sectarian fantasies. The Al-Kharrat family is multiethnic, a mixture of religions, nationalities, and language groups. Osama is of English, Armenian, and Lebanese origin. He is Druze, but his sis-ter, Lina, is a Maronite Christian. His aunt Salwa is married to Hovik, an Arme-nian. The Farouk sisters, Mariella and Fatima (who becomes Osama's wife), are Iraqi Christian and Italian Jewish. Osama and Fatima's children will therefore be of Iraqi, Italian, Jewish, Lebanese, Druze, Armenian, Chaldean, and English descent. This mixture sounds extraordinary, but it is probably no more exotic than the backgrounds to be found in most humans. Alameddine does not force this point into his readers' consciousness. Their multiethnicity is simply there, to be understood outside of their mere presence, just like the stories he tells.

Conclusion

There is so much more to discuss about Alameddine's work than I have been able to do here. Such is the case for most literary critics, especially those who are lucky enough to enjoy the literature they study. I do hope, however, that in my discussion of Alameddine's fiction I have managed to identify certain tendencies and motifs in his work. Let us take a last look at some of the more notable ones.

Alameddine's work encompasses large extended families that live in the Middle East and United States (and to a lesser extent Europe); his families are never culturally, ethnically, or philosophically homogenous; in *I, the Divine* and *The Hakawati* the families come together around a dying patriarch known for his philandering; all three novels contain a book within a book—that is, a narrative inscribed within a larger one that reflects and often supplements the novel's themes; his fiction always includes homosexual characters, Arab as well as non-Arab, and he never renders gay culture separate from Arab culture; and all of his novels explore the Lebanese Civil War in conjunction with violence, sexuality, and static worldviews. Alameddine's focus on matters of sexuality and homosexuality is especially important. Although many fiction and nonfiction writers have recently taken up these themes, Alameddine remains a pioneer in terms of raising them in a complex fashion that does not reinforce binaries or offer simplistic conclusions. Despite his often fantastical settings and story lines, we can say that Alameddine is one of the more realistic authors working today.

5

The Eternity of Immigration

Arab American Short Story Collections
(Joseph Geha, Frances Khirallah Noble,
Evelyn Shakir, Susan Muaddi Darraj)

IN THE PAST TWENTY YEARS, a number of short story collections by Arab American authors have been published. I take a look at four of those collections here: Joseph Geha's *Through and Through: Toledo Stories;* Frances Khirallah Noble's *The Situe Stories;* Evelyn Shakir's *Remember Me to Lebanon;* and Susan Muaddi Darraj's *The Inheritance of Exile.* Each collection would be an asset to a course or reading group focused on Arab American literature. Each collection resembles a novel because its stories are not discrete; the collections use recurring settings and characters, often tying them together. In total, these collections add an important dimension to the modern Arab American literary canon.

Geha, Noble, and Shakir are of Lebanese background; Muaddi Darraj is a Palestinian born in the United States. All four are Christian and write about comparable issues, though their stories and styles are far from identical. Immigration and acculturation (becoming accustomed to a different culture) are themes of note, as are negotiations of different customs and expectations, connections to the so-called Old Country, and what it means to be an "American" as opposed to an "Arab."

Joseph Geha: *Through and Through*

Through and Through: Toledo Stories is a classic of Arab American fiction. In fact, some critics (myself among them) use *Through and Through* as a demarcation point of modern Arab American literature, as opposed to the earlier period when al-Muhjar (the immigrants) predominated. Originally published in 1990 and reissued in 2009 by Syracuse University Press, *Through and Through* contains eight stories, all of them about (mainly Christian) Syro-Lebanese immigrants in Detroit and Toledo. (The term *Syro-Lebanese* refers to the period in the first half of the twentieth century when Lebanon was still a part of Syria. The immigrants from the area that would become Lebanon, in particular the largely Christian Mount Lebanon region, carried Syrian passports.) *Through and Through* explores issues of acculturation, family dynamics, and class mobility in the United States. All of the stories are realistic and utilize Aristotelian linear structures.

Although all the stories in *Through and Through* deal with the same urban setting and have characters who inhabit similar cultural terrain, they are not interconnected. The characters are not recurrent, and each story focuses on a different aspect of life in Arab Toledo, Ohio (and, in one case, Detroit). *Through and Through* is not autobiographical, but it is influenced by Geha's experience of growing up in a Lebanese immigrant community in Toledo. One of the collection's primary motifs is the way generational changes affect immigrant communities; in this case, Lebanese immigrants gradually give way to integrated Americans.

This motif is evident in "Almost Thirty," told from the point of view of Haleem Yakoub, whose grandfather Braheem was the first immigrant to the United States in his family. Braheem, Haleem, and Haleem's father, Rasheed, represent generational differences as they relate to Lebanon and the United States. Haleem explains, for instance, that Rasheed "never got used to the snow and long winters of this country."[1] Here Geha exemplifies difference through weather, a phenomenon that defines place at least as crucially as language or religion. It is not only weather that makes America different, though; the Americans themselves manage to confound and amuse the immigrants. In fact, one of the interesting features of "Almost Thirty" is the way that the Lebanese characters define "American," which appears to be coterminous with "white American" or at least with "non–Lebanese American."

These definitions become clear through the issue of marriage. The early generation of male Lebanese immigrants in "Almost Thirty," in accordance with actual history, returned to Lebanon to marry or sent for women from Lebanon to become their wives in the United States. Their children and grandchildren, however, marry "Americans." This distinction is noteworthy because we should keep in mind that the word *American* denotes nationality and not ethnicity—or at least it is supposed to denote only nationality. In other words, no matter one's ethnic, religious, or national background, one is "American" if one holds an American passport—that is to say, if one is a citizen of the United States. Haleem, Braheem, and Rasheed, then, are American. In popular culture and in America's rhetorical traditions, however, the term *American* has often been associated with whiteness and Christianity—in other words, with a certain type of American representing the majority population.

In "Almost Thirty," both the Lebanese immigrants and the Lebanese Americans appear to have internalized the latter version of American-ness. Even the American-born Haleem, who served in the navy, explains at one point, "I met an American woman, Sheila, and we were married before spring" (45). The reader will recognize that Sheila is not Lebanese because in his usage the designation *American* excludes Haleem. Haleem's uncle Habeeb "would be the first of our family to marry an American, and Aunt Afifie would refuse to go to the wedding, saying that Habeeb had become crazy like the Americans" (38). In these formulations, *American* becomes a coded term (a term whose denotation, or formal definition, differs from its predominant connotation, or popular definition). It is coded here as representative of the white, Christian majority and carries with it the presumption that an American is not only born in the United States but partakes of its various mythologies. By looking at the way these terminologies can be used, Geha helps to define his community of Lebanese American characters even as he complicates their position in the United States. Other short story writers discussed here explore the same phenomenon of national definition.

These conflicts do not get resolved as much as they work themselves out through the characters' generational development. Echoing a classic motif of American literature—that of gradual, seemingly natural assimilation—Geha's characters replace Arabic with English, tradition with individualism, and working-class origins with upward mobility. In other words, they become normatively American, according to the connotative definition. One way they accomplish this transformation is through interaction with other ethnic groups (indeed, this is the only way anybody has ever been able to engage the American polity). In "News from Phoenix," Geha explores the relationship between Arabs and Jews. The story suggests that the United States can be a productive site of interethnic dialogue. Told from the point of view of six-year-old Isaac Yakoub, "News from Phoenix" charts the progress of Sofie Yakoub, Isaac's mother, from purveyor of anti-Semitic myth to more open-minded humanist. Sofie's change results from the close relationship her family develops with the Kleins. The relationship begins as a professional one but eventually becomes personal, with the Yakoubs inviting the Kleins for dinner. Geha complicates Sofie's evolution by showing her feelings about Jews to be ambiguous, but Amos, Isaac's father, manages to transmit a more progressive perspective to his son.

Geha's characters become normatively American in other ways. One notable way they accomplish this move is through a differentiated understanding of the customs and traditions of the Old Country. The American-born characters come to view their lives in the context of what those lives would have been like had they grown up in the Middle East. In "Something Else," for example, Tonia observes that "Mama did not marry Papa for love, that part never changes. She had told Tonia what it was like in Damascus. 'He was unschooled, a stranger, as old as my father,' Mama had said. 'And I was young and pretty. It was shameful, a sin on my mother's head'" (51). In America, Tonia understands, the myth of love leading to marriage is remarkably entrenched. This differentiated view is still not enough for Tonia to feel completely American: "Tonia did not want [curly and coarse hair]. What she wanted was the tall cowgirl with smooth blond hair, also named Tonia, who came to her imagination before sleep and stayed sometimes into her dreams" (53). Tonia eventually fulfills this dream by marrying Wayne, whose mustache is "blond and barely visible" (60). Geha again shows the significance of interethnic relations in the United States: "Afterward at the reception, the band played a medley of Irish songs for Wayne's family, although he is only part Irish. Tonia sang with them" (60). For Tonia, the dream of America has been internalized in her life's reality; she has crossed enough boundaries to finally feel entrenched, one of the great ironies of Americana.

The stories in *Through and Through* are ultimately not simply about immigration and national identity; they are about complex human interaction and all the love, pain, and stimulation it creates. By focusing on these things, my intent is not to reduce the book or others similar to it to a series of sociopolitical reflections, which would be one of the more disrespectful things I could do to Arab American literature. I hope that instead I have highlighted how Geha's character conflicts exist in a particular sociopolitical context, one that problematizes what it means to be "American" and what acculturation looks like in various circumstances. The two phenomena—universal Aristotelian storytelling and sociopolitical analysis—are not opposed. In fact, they are profoundly inter-related. Geha's characters would be unable to achieve their depth of complexity without the social contexts in which they exist. Those contexts underline what it means to come to America and raise a family here, how the children of these immigrants adjust to manifold cultural expectations, and why the idea of "America" is only as strong as its inability to be easily defined.

Frances Khirallah Noble: *The Situe Stories*

Situe (pronounced "sit-tooh") is the Arabic word for "grandmother," as Frances Khirallah Noble explains at the start of *The Situe Stories,* a collection of eleven short stories that deal in some way with a *situe.* The book's title is both literal and figurative. Noble creates an array of Arabic grandmothers throughout the stories, but she also explores the *situe* as a concept and a cultural construct. In keeping with my analysis of Geha's *Through and Through,* I assess *The Situe Stories* with emphasis on how Noble invokes notions of "America" and how such a context influences the characters' interpersonal relationships.

The Situe Stories begins appropriately with a piece called "Situe," which along with the final piece, "The Honor of Her Presence," frames the collection. The pro-tagonist of these two stories is Hasna, who upon the commencement of the nar-rative has not yet become a *situe,* but who interacts with her own grandmother. As a baby, Hasna was stricken with illness, from which she eventually recovered, earning her the accolades that she was "resurrected" and "triumphant."[2] These accolades confer to Hasna a special presence, one that is almost mythical, and it is from this presence that she develops into Noble's literary matriarch. After Hasna's miraculous recovery, it does not take her long to begin challenging social conventions. On horseback, the adventurous Hasna "frightened people from the footpaths. The men said it was because she didn't have a father to contain her. The women pointed to her passive, pliant mother" (7). Without these sorts of challenges, a culture cannot evolve. Noble suggests that a strong woman is the essence of a society's ability to maintain itself and grow. Hasna cannot be catego-rized, nor can she be tamed. She defies Western expectations of subservient Arab women even while she defies the traditional norms of her own culture.

As a young adult, Hasna sets sail for the United States, her stallion in tow, at the invitation of her older brother. She never completely leaves Syria, though: "[Hasna's] Situe, on her porch, in her chair . . . felt every turn and jolt of Hasna's journey. As if she and Hasna were connected by an invisible thread" (10). On the journey, in conversation with the men of the ship, Hasna continues to surprise, first with her reflections on God, nature, and magic, noting, "Situe says they're all the same thing. And if they're not, who can tell? And if nobody can tell, what does it matter?" (12). Her other surprise is simultaneous, when, "to the astonishment of those present, Hasna lit her first pipe at sea" (12). In these scenes, Hasna is the connection among so many things: the Middle East and the United States; different generations of women; social desires and social expectations; traditional family structures and American individualism. Noble skillfully frames Hasna as the lifeblood of her stories, for Hasna makes it clear through her presence in multiple worlds that she will furnish the book's spiritual and emotional sustenance.

Once Hasna's descendants are anchored in the United States, they undertake a process of complex acculturation that resembles, though it is not identical to, that of the characters in *Through and Through*. Like Geha, Noble explores interethnic marriage. In "The War," Freddy Simon's white wife, Nora, enters into conflict with her mother-in-law, referred to simply as "Situe," who disapproves of Nora's housekeeping and mothering habits. Nora's role as a mother is a particularly divisive issue: "There were two primary bones of contention between Nora and Situe: one, how Nora took care of the baby; and two, how Nora didn't take care of the baby" (54). Noble presents this conflict as more complicated than typical (or perhaps stereotypical) mother- and daughter-in-law squabbling. There is a palpable cultural divide between Situe and Nora, one that neither person appears capable of transcending or willing to transcend. About her breastfeeding habits, for instance, Nora explains to Situe that she does it "the modern way," to which Situe responds by secretly feeding the baby cereal. Situe is unwilling to welcome Nora completely into her space because she associates Nora's habits with something alien, which she processes by associating it with Nora's physical presence.

Nora herself does not come into the relationship devoid of cultural essentialism, either. Her parents have made it difficult for her to extricate herself from negative attitudes about the culture to which Situe adheres: "Nora took [Freddy] to meet *her* family the same day she told them she and Freddy were getting married. She was pretty sure they wouldn't like him because he was Syrian and on the map it looked like Syria might be in Africa. She saw no reason to put him through the ordeal of gradual familiarity when the end result would be the same: the four of them at dinner in a restaurant to celebrate the marriage—her father cursing

Abraham Lincoln for freeing the slaves; her mother, stone-faced and sober" (55). Nora's parents are classic American racists. Freddy's Syrian family becomes implicated in that racism by virtue of their proximity to Africa, not only geographically but culturally and physically as well. Here Noble casts light on what many scholars today describe as the racialization of Arabs in the United States. Although many Arabs are identified by others and identify themselves as white, different circumstances produce identification with people of color. Freddy's situation represents one of those circumstances; he is not white enough (culturally or physically) to satisfy Nora's parents, so he automatically becomes associated with African Americans, the principal objects (along with Natives) of American racism.

Nora never actually bridges the divides she encounters and participates in. In fact, the theme of "The War" is not a conventional one of rising above difference to create understanding, but of rising above difference to create space for one's preferences. This theme becomes clear in the story's final section, when Freddy returns home from World War II and has three more children with Nora, upon which they move into the suburbs. Situe had exposed Nora's first child to a medallion bearing the image of St. Jude, as she had done when Freddy was a baby. With subsequent children, "although Nora took the medal of St. Jude with her and used it on her second child, she omitted it on the third and forth, and no one could tell the difference" (64). Nora finds a comfort zone through separation (from Situe and her traditions), not through dialogue. This distinction is important because it emphasizes the fundamental discrepancies that often create conflict among immigrants to the United States and the rooted populations with whom they interact.

Perhaps the story that best exemplifies the complexity of assimilation is "The American Way." Many writers and scholars throughout the years have questioned what it is that immigrants are supposed to assimilate into. There is no singular American culture, after all, even if popular media try to convince us otherwise. We have a mythology of the suburban home, picket fence, and patriotic commitment, a firmly white and middle-class image, but in reality there are thousands of different ways to be American and to participate in the ceremonies of the United States. One way to be American, Noble illustrates in "The American Way," is to adhere to a form of capitalism that values the end result of success more than it does the means through which success is achieved. Or, to put it more simply, the story illustrates that one important component of the American dream is to get paid by hook or by crook. The protagonist of "The American Way," Mansour Malouf, finds an excellent and quintessentially "American" way to get paid.

Echoing some of the mythical tactics of American mafia, Mansour, with the blessing of his more successful older brother and disabled brother-in-law, Jimmy, starts an illegal gambling operation. He needs money to cover his debts as a result of his own gambling habit and to supplement his wife's materialism. His decision is replete with symbolic meaning. First, it reproduces a particular American ethos that equates business prowess and earning potential with manhood. "A man at last," Mansour's older brother thinks to himself when Mansour pitches the idea to him (85). Mansour is not worthy of respect as a real man until he is willing to take the necessary risks, legal or not, to become financially successful. His pursuit of an illegal gambling operation also places him in a grand tradition of immigrant outlaws that has become quintessentially American. At one point, the police discover an after-hours card game and, having decided not to arrest the offenders, ask, "Say . . . you guys Italian . . . or what?" (94). This question firmly ensconces the gamblers in a mythological American discourse, suggesting that they are mafia. They end up fulfilling that mythological discourse by paying off the police and by developing an elaborate system of managing the operation's finances.

A particularly interesting American mythology is exposed in a line Mansour's older brother uses in response to Mansour's lingering nervousness about his proposed enterprise: "This country rewards ingenuity. And hard work. I know. I started with nothing. And look where I am now. I seized the opportunity in front of me. Now you do the same. It's the American way" (87). It is true that American-style capitalism rewards ingenuity and hard work; it was set up to reward these qualities. However, implicit in its value system is the notion that making money is ultimately more important than economic honesty. Respect, we all know, is afforded the wealthy even when they did or do unsavory things to acquire their wealth. Mansour's brother responds to this fact, providing Mansour with a realistic assessment of his responsibility as an immigrant (which is to live the American dream by making as much money as possible). It is through the paradoxical strategy of working within the system even while defying it that Mansour decides to fulfill the promise of America. He earns his money (and the attendant respect), but he also takes on the anxiety that accompanies upward mobility in the United States.

In this way, *The Situe Stories* explores the terrain of belonging in America. Noble portrays the United States as a place of productive instability—that is, a place where nobody actually follows expectations and protocols and everybody thus manages to provide his or her own contribution to national identity as a result. Noble's focus on the *situe* as moral and thematic center of her fiction illuminates the importance of women in both American and Middle Eastern cultures, the primacy of women in building the United States, and the salience of imparting wisdom from elders to youth. *The Situe Stories* demands that readers examine the spaces in the United States and the Middle East that do not always merit attention from those who like to constrict American and Arab identities.

Evelyn Shakir: *Remember Me to Lebanon*

Remember Me to Lebanon represents Lebanese American Evelyn Shakir's entrée into the genre of fiction. Shakir is a seminal critic of Arab American culture and literature, in particular the histories of Arab American women. These interests are reflected in *Remember Me to Lebanon,* a collection of ten short stories that is subtitled *Stories of Lebanese Women in America.* Though the subtitle is accurate, it is slightly misleading in that some of the women Shakir examines are not Lebanese and she sometimes writes from the point of view of male characters.

The bulk of the stories deal with Lebanese American women, however. These women are of varied ages, but they share a few things in common: they live in Boston, have relationships with multiple cultures, and defy stereotype. Like Toledo in Geha's stories, Boston in *Remember Me to Lebanon* is an additional character, playing an important role in the sense of place underlying and sometimes guiding the action. Shakir takes care to create a vibrant Bostonian setting that gives her fiction a distinctive presence. Her Boston is mainly working class and multiethnic. The stories range in time from the 1960s to the present.

Like other Arab American fiction, Shakir's work uses some archetypal themes (which certainly are not limited to Arab American writing): cultural conflict among Eastern immigrants and white Americans; the foundational role of women in Arab American society; anti-Arab racism and Islamophobia; and the anxieties of maintaining an identity in the United States. All of these themes can be found in "The Trial," a story that does not actually contain any courtroom scenes. The title refers instead to trials of emotional and cultural import. A single-narrator story, "The Trial" follows sixty-nine-year-old Sadie as she embarks on a routine trip to her house from the grocery store that turns out to have an unusual glitch.

That glitch arrives in the form of a person, the elderly Lillian, who appears to be disoriented or perhaps even delusional. Lillian accosts Sadie, much to Sadie's displeasure, and in their ensuing conversation a number of symbolic themes arise. "The Trial" illuminates issues of memory, location, and belonging in immigrant communities. In her ostensible ramblings, Lillian manages to center Sadie in a firm sense of place, an irony that exposes Sadie's own tenuous understanding of reality. One way Lillian accomplishes this irony is through her very presence, which Sadie cannot escape because it activates her reluctant sense of responsibility. Lillian, in other words, does not allow Sadie the freedom to go about her business alone. Lillian, however, does not physically accost or verbally intimidate Sadie; Sadie ultimately chooses to entertain Lillian's delusions not because she finds them pleasant, but because she disallows herself the option of merely walking away, a fundamentally ethical decision.

The symbolism of "The Trial" also produces an important subtext, one that illuminates Sadie and Lillian's closeness despite Sadie's reluctance to admit this fact. Lillian embodies one of Sadie's greatest fears: abandonment and lack of agency. (In literary study, the term *agency* generally refers to one's ability to be self-represented, powerful enough to make his or her own decisions, and situated in a clear-cut social position.) This recognition comes to fruition when Lillian's nephew, Emile, finally tracks her down, explaining to Sadie, "We made an appointment for her, tomorrow with a specialist. She doesn't want to go, she's scared of doctors. But it's not up to her, is it?"[3] Emile's comment arrives on the heels of an unpleasant memory Sadie has just considered, of when she moved her ailing mother into a nursing home: "'I had to,'" Sadie explained to herself and to anyone who'd listen. In those last weeks when her mother was still with her, all night Sadie had been afraid to sleep. In case her mother got out of bed and fell. And even with Sadie's help, she might not make it to the bathroom in time. Sadie remembered the diapers she'd resorted to and the accidents on the rug. 'I'll visit you every day,' she'd promised. And she had. And later in the hospital. 'God punish you,' her mother had said" (102). Sadie's mother was in a condition not unlike Lillian's in that they both have lost their agency. Sadie's mother was mentally coherent, though, whereas Lillian appears to be physically strong. The burden of age and the loss of skills ring similar to Sadie, and she is forced to confront her own place within familial and communal environments. Ultimately, though, she heeds the symbolic lessons to which Lillian has introduced her: "Good thing, she had companions. Uncle on one side of her, Auntie on the other. She was glad now she hadn't bought a whole quart of jam. As she told them, it would have been more than she could carry. They murmured something. They seemed to understand" (104). Sadie does not necessarily assume a new outlook toward the world, but she definitely learns to focus on carrying the items of her life in a more realistic and comfortable fashion.

"The Trial," like many of the stories, does not focus explicitly on Arab American ethnicity (though that ethnicity is certainly an element in the story, as it is throughout the collection). One story, however, manages to incorporate the poetic signatures that define Shakir's style while offering pointed commentary on contemporary sociopolitical issues. "I've Got My Eye on You" is simultaneously a story about an elderly woman and her inner conflicts and an exploration of the culture of surveillance that grew up in the United States following the events of September 11, 2001. The narrator, a white American woman, is lonely, and in her loneliness she likes to keep abreast of the goings-on in her neighborhood. Her favorite person to monitor is thirteen-year-old Sissie, an Arab Muslim girl whose family, it seems to the narrator, is perpetually up to something (142).

It is not just Sissie's family that invokes the narrator's suspicion. She explains that the entire neighborhood feels somehow different and less safe than in the old days, "when the Muellers and the Mahoneys lived next door" (132). Given the context of this comment, readers are meant to understand that the Muellers and the Mahoneys were white, unlike the "strangers" now surrounding the nostalgic narrator. The entire story is filled with this type of subtext, where the narrator and her sister, Tillie, mix homegrown xenophobia with anxieties about a range of fantastical scenarios (involving terrorist plots and strange, secret rituals) that are not totally outlandish given the way the sisters have been made to understand Arabs and Muslims in popular culture. For instance, when the narrator and Tillie, who refer to the neighbors casually as "the terrorists," discuss Sissie's mother, the narrator notes, "They're not Arabs through and through. . . . The mother doesn't cover up, maybe just a scarf around her hair," to which Tillie responds, "That shows they're crafty. . . . They want to melt right in" (132). Here the narrator and Tillie create an image of Arabs based on sensationalistic assumptions and in turn judge their credibility based on their conformity to those images, without thinking to interact with the Arabs themselves.

The narrator is not the only one concerned with eyes. When Sissie and her cousin Mohammad ("Mo") lock themselves out of Sissie's house, Sissie brings Mo to the narrator's house and asks if he can use her bathroom, to which the narrator reluctantly agrees. Mo's presence in her home evokes the narrator's paranoia (which does not appear to be limited simply to Arabs). In her obsessive-compulsive haste to clean the bathroom upon Mo's departure from it, she discovers a "tiny little oval thing. Like a girl's charm almost, but wood around the edge and in the middle a stone painted like an eye. A blue eye, if you please" (137). This charm is common among Middle Eastern cultures and is used to ward off the evil eye; people carry the charm as an American might carry a rabbit's foot, or, more commonly, they hang it inside their homes. (You may recall that Rabih Alameddine tells the story of Fatima's hand and the evil eye in *The Hakawati*. One of Susan Muaddi Darraj's stories also uses the symbolism of the evil eye.)

Sensing its power, the narrator wants nothing to do with Mo's amulet and covers it with a tissue, a move that draws a rebuke from Sissie and anger from Mo, who informs the narrator that if "[you're] asking for [trouble], you'll get it" (138). The narrator is not looking for trouble as much as she is attempting to avoid it. Her methods of avoidance unfortunately invoke the very problems she purports to avoid. Shakir draws on the mythology of the amulet when Mo points out that the narrator's eyes are blue, the color of evil that the blue amulet must repel. Her blue eye is trained on Mo: "Every ten minutes by my watch, I've been dialing [Sissie's house]. When Sissie answers, I hang up. Just making sure she's not laying on her back—saints forgive me for what I'm thinking—that big fellow over her, and the brother standing watch" (140). This passage reflects a number of social phenomena in the United States, most evidently fear of the lustful Arab male, who, according to stereotype, has a voracious sexual appetite and lacks the impulse (or intelligence or moral acumen) to control it. This oversexed male does not value women and therefore presents a constant threat to them. The narrator of "I've Got My Eye on You" is both responding to this sort of imagery vis-à-vis Mo and imposing that imagery on him.

After working herself into an adequate paranoia, with some help from Tillie, the narrator calls 911, ironically because she is disturbed that her neighbors are spying on her. Shakir closes the story with a vivid touch, focusing on the smugly defensive but satisfied narrator watching the happy gathering next door as police lights appear on the street. "Never dreaming what's gonna hit," she thinks (144). Shakir employs a literary technique of textual irony in which the audience knows something of which the characters are unaware. This particular irony is heartbreaking as Sissie's joyous extended family is about to have its merriment unexpectedly interrupted. Shakir does not tell readers what the specific consequences of the police visit will be, but readers can infer that they will not be positive. Beyond being an exploration of character conflict, "I've Got My Eye on You" is an allegory of the culture of citizen spying and pervasive suspiciousness in American society. This culture existed before September 11 but has been accelerated in its aftermath. Without being pedantic, Shakir illuminates the dangers of submitting to the fear that is programmed into Americans through news broadcasts and political commentaries. Moreover, she illuminates who that danger most affects: innocent Arab Americans who become a victim of their fellow citizens' logical response to what it now means to act patriotically.

All of the stories in *Remember Me to Lebanon* explore various character conflicts that render the collection highly personal; many of them also contextualize those conflicts with social issues that situate the characters within the broader events that affect their lives (and the readers' lives). Like Geha and Noble's work, Shakir's is realistic and focused on a chronological structure, though many of the themes she examines are distinct from those raised by comparable writers (e.g., the complexities of aging, the symbolic importance of basic human interaction, the ever-changing landscape of Americana). And although I would characterize Shakir's fiction as political, as I would all fiction, it is political in a different way than our next writer's.

Susan Muaddi Darraj: *The Inheritance of Exile*

The primary reason that I deem Susan Muaddi Darraj's politics different than Shakir's has nothing to do with the orientation of those politics (which might be exactly the same, for all I know—but do not actually know). The difference exists in how those politics are expressed and in the political context of the writing itself. Much of the politics of *Remember Me to Lebanon* is expressed allegorically; although Muaddi Darraj also employs some allegorical structures, her politics are more explicitly stated and more inscribed in the progression of some of her short stories. *The Inheritance of Exile* is both a political document and an example of skillfully crafted aesthetics. Or we might view it as an integration of the two.

I have saved my analysis of Muaddi Darraj until last not because I like her work least or best (I like the work of all four authors, though my personal reaction is not supposed to matter). I have positioned her here because I find important distinctive qualities about both author and text that I would like to assess briefly vis-à-vis Geha, Noble, and Shakir. First of all, Muaddi Darraj is not Lebanese, but Palestinian, so she emphasizes a slightly different set of geopolitical and cultural phenomena. Moreover, she is invested in the cultural politics of race and ethnicity in the United States, a discussion that Palestinian Americans have participated in heavily during the past decade. Finally, she presents a narrative structure that is more integrated than in the other three titles.

The Inheritance of Exile does share important similarities with the other three titles, however: a setting largely within an urban environment; an exploration of place as an additional character; a look into variegated cultural conflicts and their heterogeneous aftermaths; a focus on difficult matters around assimilation and acculturation; a fictive analysis of what it means to be "American"; a frank representation of the difficulties and sometimes joys of intercultural marriage; and an almost exclusive use of women protagonists, a textual element not found in *Through and Through*.

Rather than reinventing the wheel by examining in Muaddi Darraj's book what I have critiqued already in the other three, I would like to extend the range of my overall discussion by pointing to some of the issues in *The Inheritance of Exile* that render it distinct, in particular Muaddi Darraj's treatment of cultural politics and her structural presentation, which makes the book feel just as much like a novel as a short story collection. Let me begin with the second point. It seems to me that each piece in *The Inheritance of Exile* can stand alone as a discrete story, but at the same time, taken together, they are interrelated in such a way that each becomes richer in the presence of the others. This is so because the setting in a working-class Philadelphia is continuous, and the characters reappear throughout the collection. The characters actually do more than simply reappear; they also do not progress through chronological time, providing *The Inheritance of Exile* with what literary critics call "multiple perspectivism"—a retelling of the same episodes through different points of view.

Four women—Nadia, Aliyah, Hanan, and Reema—narrate the stories, though Muaddi Darraj provides their mothers with their own points of view. Nadia, Aliyah, and Hanan are Christian, Reema a Muslim. The would-be religious division does not materialize, and Muaddi Darraj points to the historical interreligious harmony among Palestinians, both in the Arab world and in the United States. The women are roughly the same age and have known each other since they were children. There are two layers of stories in *The Inheritance of Exile*, one layer focusing on the friendship among the mothers (Siham is Nadia's mother; Lamis [Imm Nabil] is Aliyah's mother; Layla is Hanan's mother; Huda is Reema's mother). The other layer focuses on the daughters' friendship and travails as they age and move into their individual lives. These layers create something of a structural tapestry that is not necessarily patterned but is interconnected.

One sensibility that binds all the women is a focus on safety—not just physical safety, but cultural and financial safety as well. Siham, for instance, hangs blue evil eye amulets throughout her home, not only recalling the devotion of Sissie's cousin Mo in Shakir's story, but also symbolizing a profound desire for a safe and familiar space in a strange and colossal America. In another moment, Hanan notes of her mother, Layla, "Mama had stopped trusting anyone who was American, anyone who could possibly be a criminal."[4] Layla expresses this sort of sentiment elsewhere, as do most of the other characters, indicating that they continue to draw a sharp distinction between the culture of Palestine and the culture of the United States. This distinction inspires a number of conflicts centered around either cultural differences or predetermined (and stubborn) definitions of "Arab" and "American."

Layla's distrust of "Americans," for example, is sincere and has a particular context, so I would consider it unfair to minimize that distrust. At the same time, though, it is fundamentally illogical because she employs a usage of "American" that recalls the ambiguities of its use in the fiction of Geha, Noble, and Shakir. Layla herself is an American, as is her daughter, only she does not see them in this light because she invests a normative American identity with ethnological features that assume a white cultural orientation. In another example, Aliyah explains to Nadia that a potential love interest she meets in Jerusalem "wants me to be less American" (36). In another story, Layla describes her relationship with her Arab American husband using an ethnicized language: "I try to be sufficiently Arab, but just American enough for him." One of the ways in which she acts adequately American is revealing: she learns "to fry chicken without burning it" (102). (She also develops a taste for Bruce Springsteen.)

It is these dueling versions of American-ness and Arabness that underpin the majority of interpersonal conflicts in the book. Those conflicts involve seemingly mundane scenes that represent broader problems (e.g., Hanan sopping her food up with bread to the horror of her white fiancé's parents); they also involve crucial scenes whose problems are obvious (e.g., Hanan's not wanting to be exoticized by her husband's pretentious academic colleagues or Reema's being asked stupid things by her boyfriend about Muslim polygamy and being referred to as his "harem girl"). In fact, although Reema occupies the least amount of space in *The Inheritance of Exile*, she encounters the most conspicuous instances of racism. Her boyfriend, Alex, excitedly rents the 1921 Rudolph Valentino film *The Sheik*, an early example of Hollywood racism against Arabs. Reema identifies what to her are obvious problems with the film, but Alex fails to see them, deciding that he and Reema will simply have to agree to disagree. Yet Reema "didn't see *how* he could agree to disagree, because you cannot disagree about something that's incorrect" (174). Reema views the racism in *The Sheik* as a simple fact, whereas Alex believes that racism is a matter of perception, a position that only those who have never experienced racism would believe. A large part of Reema's revulsion to *The Sheik* arises from her past, when she was called epithets such as *towelhead* and *camel jockey* in school. Muaddi Darraj does not explicitly juxtapose the film with the casual racism of Reema's classmates, but she indicates to readers that the two phenomena are not discrete.

A less explicit but no less important example of ethnic reckoning can be found throughout the long section dealing with Hanan and her failed marriage. Hanan and her husband, John Martin, a sociologist, do not break up because of unbridgeable cultural differences. They break up because of more general—and common—factors: conflicts between Hanan and her in-laws; different visions of the future; a lack of fundamental trust in one another's level of devotion. Cultural differences nevertheless play a role in the existence of those factors. At a sociology department soirée in which John plays the role of sycophant in order to increase his chances of earning a tenure-track position, his and Hanan's latent problems become overt, in part because Hanan does not want to be pigeonholed into a narrow ethnic posture. It turns out that John's pretentious department chair is doing research on Arab women and asks Hanan to read her manuscript. When Hanan asks her why, she answers, "Well, for *authenticity*. I want an Arab woman's per-spective on how *real* my writing is, how genuine and *accurate* my observations." Hanan's response surprises everybody: "But, but I'm not Arab" (139).

Hanan is not disavowing her ethnic background as much as she is drawing a distinction between her experience and the experiences of those about whom the professor wishes to write. She does not feel qualified to speak on behalf of women who were born and raised in the Middle East, a place she has never even visited, nor is she willing to trade in her American identity for a Middle Eastern one, as the professor's request tacitly forces her to do. These choices rely on a firm distinction between "Arab" and "American," one that need not be rigid. Hanan makes it rigid in the context of her reaction to the professor, which indicates that her own sense of identity is incomplete, further evidenced by the fact that she does know which word to use to describe Palestine. At the soirée, it becomes clear that all of John's colleagues want somebody exotic, a role Hanan is unwilling to play (she makes it a point to inform one person that she was born in Philadel-phia). When John later informs her that he wishes she would have played that role to help him achieve his career ambitions, Hanan begins to view him in a fundamentally different way.

Although the stories are replete with similar conflicts around cultural and personal expectations, Muaddi Darraj creates other themes within and beyond Arab American culture. Two of those themes within Arab American culture are the uses of food as a fictive motif and the immanence of Palestine in Arab Ameri-can political consciousness. (In chapter 7, I look at how Arab American writers explore the Palestine question.) Let us start with Palestine. Although I would not describe *The Inheritance of Exile* as either pedantic or overtly political, Muaddi Darraj does not eschew politics altogether. She incorporates the issue of Palestine realistically, illuminating how it has become an everyday factor, culturally and politically, in the lives of Arab Americans, those of Palestinian origin especially. In the collection, Muaddi Darraj renders Palestine an omnipresent space that provides meaning to the characters' habits and characteristics and highlights the pain that has come with dispossession. This space is particularly apparent when the mothers reflect on their childhoods in refugee camps.

Muaddi Darraj's use of food motifs is also illuminative of a particular cul-tural disposition. Food evokes togetherness, invokes the characters' heritage, and embodies many of the qualities associated with Palestine. The inclusion of food motifs has been common throughout the history of ethnic and immigrant American writing. Muaddi Darraj follows a long line of writers, Arab American and otherwise, who explore the interrelation of food with culture and geography. In the other short story collections we have looked at in this chapter, for instance, food is an integral part of each collection's cultural exposition. The interesting thing about Muaddi Darraj's use of the motif is not the presence of food itself, but the fact that she manages to make food a central element of the narrative without allowing it to dictate the characters' identities and thus to become a cliché. As with everything else in the stories, she integrates food motifs into a wider setting around generational and cultural conflicts under which the narrative conventions are subsumed.

Muaddi Darraj also integrates different cultural apparatuses throughout her collection. She does not appear content to draw a firm line between Arab and American cultures. This move is apparent in the relationship between daughters and mothers who have to compromise on some deeply held viewpoint in order to grow and coexist. Although the characters do not always succeed in creating new ground for the development of new cultures, they frequently manage to accommodate one another in ways that are both subtle and explicit. In one scene, this ability to create new ground occurs, appropriately enough, through the innovative use of food: "[John] sat down at our small kitchen table and started spreading peanut butter and jelly on a slice of pita bread. It was the marriage of Arab and American food—like hummus on a hoagie" (130).

Conclusion: Transcendental Grandmothers

The grandmother in Arab American literature endeavors to transcend: she is never sectarian; she does not transmit negative elements of Arab culture; and she exemplifies the strength of womanhood, both Middle Eastern and otherwise. The Arab grandmother is sometimes romanticized, but she often acts as a metonym of the Arab spirit of resilience. Modern Arab American writing, in particular the works of its formative years in the 1990s, is filled with deployments of this character. Much recent fiction, including Muaddi Darraj's, eschews the sort of aesthetic that is generally produced by a focus on the Arab grandmother, which is what I would call "microcultural" (invested in the nuances of everyday and interpersonal culture). The history of the Arab grandmother in Arab American writing is a rich one, but it is changing with the emergence of new writers and the different focuses they bring to the genre. But as we have seen, it is a focus that still exists in the genre of the short story, in particular those produced by Lebanese American authors.

Issues and styles other than the ones I have discussed exist in the short stories examined here. Part of their heterogeneity arises from the fact that Arab culture is not monolithic, but a series of different customs, traditions, and worldviews, sometimes at odds and sometimes in harmony. The literature of Arab America reflects those differences. According to the poet and critic Lisa Suhair Majaj, the diversity of audiences for whom Arab Americans write also affects the evolution of the writing: "When we write and publish, we speak both to and for Arab-Americans and we address as well readers both within and without of our many other communities—national, gendered, cultural, political, and literary. This diversity of readers has a significant impact on how and what we write."[5] Majaj's statement is a good way to acknowledge that Arab American fiction complicates not only simplistic notions of Arab culture, but also simplistic explanations of how Arab culture interacts with the thousands of other cultures in the United States.

6

Promised Lands and Unfulfilled Promises

Laila Halaby

LAILA HALABY HAS WRITTEN two novels, *West of the Jordan* and *Once in a Promised Land,* that have been well received critically and have earned a steady readership. Both novels focus on a range of sociopolitical issues involving Arab American identity, civil liberties, racism and xenophobia, and the effects of September 11, 2001, on American society. It is easy to read Halaby only in the context of the political events that frame or appear in her fiction, but there is a great deal happening aesthetically in her novels, so I would like to be careful not to reduce art solely to political commentary. Halaby does comment on the state of affairs in the United States, however—a dimension of her fiction that is difficult to avoid. Here, I try to situate those comments within an analysis of her poetic structures.

Halaby is an Arizona-based writer of Palestinian Jordanian and white American background. ("Palestinian Jordanian" refers to the majority population of Jordan, which is from 60 to 70 percent of Palestinian origin.) Her worldly background leads her to transnational settings, but her main geographical focus is Arizona, California, Jordan, and the West Bank of Palestine. Both of her novels examine the social and cultural positions of Palestinians in the United States. Of particular note is her identification and exploration of the spaces between American promises and the difficult realities that quietly exist alongside them.

West of the Jordan

West of the Jordan is a title that denotes both geography and political orientation. On the one hand, it directs readers' attention to the West Bank and to the geopolitical West, the United States in particular. On the other hand, it identifies a locus of concerns that combine an emphasis on the United States and the Middle East. Four teenage women, all first cousins, narrate the novel; each young woman represents a different cultural, historical, and economic situation. In the case of Mawal, she also represents a different locale, the West Bank town of Nawara, from which the Salaama family hails. Although each narrator's personality is distinct, they all share the presence of Palestine as a crucial source of their identities. Khadija illuminates religious conservatism and male angst; Soraya represents the amoral waywardness of the United States and conflicts over individuality and community; Hala, arguably the novel's main protagonist, negotiates a series of transnational questions; and Mawal is a metaphorical anchor, the culturally grounded, responsible keeper of stories.

Mawal also creates the novel's broadest metaphor, the *roza,* an intricately embroidered Palestinian dress, each pattern representing a different site in Palestine. At one point, Mawal says, "Stories are stitched under the skin at birth."[1] Mawal stitches *roza*s to honor her ancestors and to remember her community's past. The patterns she creates come to denote the interrelation of the novel's characters. They further denote the characters' connection to Nawara. As the threads connect themselves to the fabric, the characters become indivisible from their place of ancestry. Mawal serves as the other three characters' foil in that she reminds them of what they once were and what they were close to becoming. Her mantra when embroidering embodies the novel's metaphorical values:

> Stitch in red for life.
> Stitch in green to remember.
> Stitch, stitch to never forget. (103)

If Mawal has an opposite, it would have to be Soraya, the Los Angeles–based teenager who is sexually active, cynical, and ambiguous beneath her hyperconfident exterior. A critic might analyze Soraya in many ways, but I would like to focus on the role she plays in undermining mythologies about America and the American dream. Many of the immigrants in *West of the Jordan,* reflecting the attitudes of many real-life immigrants, view the United States as a stable place that holds the promise of a specific trajectory: arrival, hard work, slowly accumulated wealth, family and comfortable home, children who outdo parents' success. Nonimmigrant Americans often adhere to a comparable but slightly different mythology, one that casts the United States as a secure but perpetually threatened site of economic possibility and ethical exceptionalism. (The notion of American exceptionalism claims that the United States is an exceptional force of good in the world and that no other nation can match its freedoms and its inventiveness.)

Soraya challenges both of these tidy narratives. Because she manages to complicate the myths of Americana and exposes the various forms of denial that accompany those myths, she achieves a richness that inevitably makes her controversial for reasons other than her promiscuity and her bizarre sexual relationship with her uncle Hamdan (a relationship that denotes a fetishization of familial bonding and a sexualization of male power). A good example of such controversy arises in the scene Soraya recounts about Sameer Samaha, a hardworking immigrant who is supposedly murdered in a random mugging, but whose death Soraya deems suspicious, theorizing instead that the honest Sameer was a victim of his wife's unfaithfulness. Soraya suspects that Sameer walked in on Suad and her lover and was subsequently murdered; Suad then invented the story about the random mugger. It is a fantastical theory, but not completely unrealistic. However, it is Soraya's conclusion, not her theory, that resonates: "So that is what you get for Working Your Ass Off and then trying to be traditional" (95). She is expressing more than disdain here; she is questioning the assumption that in the United States hard work and honesty will ensure success and stability. Her method of vocalization is rather crass, but her conclusion is actually more realistic than the mythology's promise.

Soraya challenges the veracity of the American dream in other ways, too. Her remarkably eventful life leads her into unusual and sometimes dangerous situations. While at a "white" bar with her cousin Walid, for instance, she responds to racist encroachments by proclaiming, "We're Americans," a fact that proves too difficult for their tormentors to acknowledge (59). The racists eventually beat up Walid and direct more invective at Soraya. The scene provides a simple enough commentary on racism and belonging but manages to become fully relevant through the different uses of the term *American* that produce the confrontation and its subsequent violence. Soraya and Walid's presence in the bar as "Mexicans," symbolic of an amorphous brown non-American in the bar patrons' minds, is objectionable in itself, but it does not induce violence until the moment of Soraya's proclamation that she and Walid are American. The attackers then feel as if they are protecting their sanctified turf and upholding the mythology of a whiteness that presupposes a proper American identity. Soraya later understands the role Arabs play in these American mythologies: "Still wishing . . . that I were a superhero like in those cartoons where she comes in and wipes out the bad guys and still looks good. But there aren't any Arab ones, are there? My hair is too dark, too thick; my skin is too far away from white to let me even pretend to be an American superhero" (60).

Soraya's comprehension of how such mythologies are rooted is not always to her detriment. She is a trickster in her high school, often fascinating her gullible classmates: "I tell them what they want to hear, which is nasty stories about young men sticking their things into goats and some twelve-year-old girl being carried off on a camel to be third wife to old Shaykh So-and-So and the five oil wells my father owns" (24). Her exasperated mother cannot understand why she would reinforce such outrageous stereotypes, something Soraya never bothers to explain. Her opening line, "I have fire," reveals more than just hyperbole. It indicates that Soraya is infused with light and passion, that she has the rare ability to bring people together or to scatter them away. Her tricksterism in school is most obviously for her sheer amusement, but, more important, it indicates her refusal to be docile or subservient. She fulfills stereotypes because it gives her power over her classmates rather than enabling those stereotypes to exert power over her. Soraya has learned how to use the exclusionary American dream to her advantage.

Khadija is paradoxically most like and most different from Soraya. She is most like Soraya in that both of them deal with the same cultural conflicts at home and in school. Her problems begin with elemental issues. "In America," she explains, "my name sounds like someone throwing up or falling off a bicycle" (36). These problems seem to be pervasive in school. Even her friendly teacher, Mr. Napolitano, uses what Khadija finds to be an unacceptable conception of American-ness: "He expects me to know more than the other kids because my parents are not American, though there are lots of other kids in the class who aren't Americans themselves. I want to scream at him that I am just as American as anyone here" (74). Home offers her no respite. "No! No daughter of mine is American," her mother screams when Khadija points out this obvious reality (74). When Khadija attempts to integrate herself into American life by striking up a friendship with her classmate Patsy, she learns just how much her Palestinian cultural background has shaped her worldly outlook. She notes with a mixture of shock and regret that going to Patsy's house for dinner "was like walking into a TV show" (150). Although Khadija is amused that Patsy's brother, Mickey, is named after Mick Jagger, Khadija's mother is less impressed: "*This* is the problem with America! Instead of naming their children after family or prophets or heroes, they name them after rock stars. Who would believe such a thing?" (151).

Khadija's issues are also deeply troublesome, and here is where she becomes most different from Soraya. She deals most particularly with her father's abusiveness, which he attributes to his failed American dream. Khadija explains that her father "has many dreams that have been filled with sand. That's what he tells me: 'This country has taken my dreams that used to float like those giant balloons, and filled them with sand. Now they don't float, and you can't even see what they are anymore'" (37). Khadija's father, a part-time mechanic, is an alcoholic and sometimes physically abusive. He is not only the poorest of the male immigrants in the novel, but also the most religious. Halaby does not directly tie together his poverty and his religiosity, but it is reasonable to infer that the two are related, even if not causally. His abusiveness comes to a head when in a drunken fit he attacks his father and baby son, prompting Khadija to call the police, an act that causes her to fear that she will be blamed for breaking up the family.

Khadija's story does not have a happy ending, a fact that in itself undermines a cherished American mythology. She becomes symbolic of the conflicts that exist among strict religious devotion, free-market capitalism, immigration, and disparate cultural norms and values. It might be unfair to say that Khadija is trapped within conflicting impulses and traditions, but she certainly occupies a position that appears to demand conflicting loyalties. This demand arises from her age, life as a high school student, multilingual and cultural identity, and working-class status. The reality of Khadija's life barely conforms to the image of what her life is supposed to be. Uncomfortable with her "American" friends and equally uncomfortable at home, she attempts to reconcile different elements of her life that simply will not acquiesce to being reconciled. If they did, then everybody's lives in the United States would be much less complicated.

If any of the characters represents stability, it is Mawal, whose location in Palestine is not incidental to that perceived stability. Beyond her role as the keeper of stories and history, Mawal observes the lives of her American cousins from a position of ignorance because she does not receive firsthand news about events in the United States, only gossip and secondhand tales. This position confers to her a certain power, though, because it enables her to assess these events without being embroiled in them. Having no particular stake in their outcomes, she manages to engage America without succumbing to its inevitable contradictions.

Mawal also has the misfortune of spatial and political limitations that do not affect her American counterparts. She deals with Israeli checkpoints and other indignities of the occupation of the West Bank. These realities play a role in determining the sort of worldview Mawal develops and the particular outlook toward the United States—a mixture of fascination and resentment—that can be found throughout her narration. At one point, she complains, "You would think our village was in love with America with all the people who have left, like America is the best relative in the world that everyone has to visit. America is more like a greedy neighbor who takes the best out of you and leaves you feeling empty" (96). Her observation reveals her politics and her personality. Her politics are oriented around pride in ancestry and an investment in the Palestinian landscape, an emphasis she shares with (or learned from) her grandmother: "'No matter what our difficulties, it is better here,' she would always say" (96). This statement highlights a person who takes seriously her commitment to communal sustenance: the migration from Nawara not only breaks apart the Salaamas' close family structure but also suggests enough displeasure with Palestine to allow it to become less important than the United States. Mawal is unhappy that émigrés profess a deep allegiance to Palestine but vote with their feet, so to speak, in taking their talents elsewhere.

Hala exists in both the Middle East and America, so she acts as a symbolic bridge between the two spaces culturally, politically, and physically. She has a Jordanian father and grew up in Jordan, but as a teenager she immigrated to the United States—Arizona, specifically—to study at the urging of her Palestinian mother. As she prepares to depart to Jordan at the start of the novel, she remembers how she felt when she immigrated: "I was terrified at the thought of being away from my family, even though the idea of going to America—the America my mother had only tasted—*was* exciting" (9). In this passage, Hala underlines one of the novel's central social themes—a distinction Laila Halaby makes between America as an actual physical space and the idea of "America," a set of mythologies, promises, and dreamscapes. The idea of America has been its great attraction, one that Soraya and Khadija struggle with, but the actual nation-state of America entails sacrifices and demands that are not advertised in its mythologies.

Halaby interweaves these American dualities with the mythologies and promises of the Middle East through the character of Hala (and, in a different way, through Mawal). Hala notices these contradictions immediately, and they make the distance between Jordan and the United States seem irreconcilable. During her first week in Jordan, she observes, "There *is* comfort to be in my own house, to wake up in my own language, but all those faces I've carried with me for so long wear suspicion in their eyes as they greet me. I have walked so far away from them" (77). Hala finds herself in a state of liminality, an existence in different spaces without feeling completely whole in either—an in-between state of being, to put it more simply. Her liminality is both enhanced and challenged by Sharif Abdel-Hameed, a Palestinian Jordanian suitor (and distant cousin) who comes to embody the Middle East to Hala. Sharif exists in her past and becomes indivisible in her mind from the mystique (and mythology) of Palestine, a position that becomes clear when she reflects on a childhood trip she took to Aqaba, a port/resort town in the far south of Jordan on the Red Sea.

Aqaba occupies a small stretch of land bordered on the tip of the Red Sea by Israel, Egypt, and Saudi Arabia, all of which can be seen easily from Jordan. As Hala remembers, in a paddle boat a considerable distance from shore Sharif pulled her toward Palestine, at which point they were stopped by Jordanian officials, who laughingly informed them that the Israelis would not let them land in Eilat, the Israeli port/resort town on the Red Sea. The scene reinforces the inability to return "home," a particularly hurtful realization for Palestinians, as Hala indicates, especially given the fact that even water, a more fluid topography than land, can be monitored and policed as if it has a fixed border. Palestine thus becomes symbolic of the characters' liminality; it is a visible physical presence, but one that cannot be accessed and therefore one that takes on extraterritorial dimensions (that is, it becomes much larger than its physical borders). When older family members asked Hala where she had intended to go, she shouted, "We tried to go home!" (129). She later remembers this scene with an intimate comfort: "That is the sweet picture in my mind as I drift off to sleep, surrounded by my mother's presence" (129). This sort of emphasis in a Halaby novel is unsurprising. She noted in an interview that "Palestine has always been central to my writing. Love of land, loss, exile, forcible removal, the physical beauty of land being bittersweet because it is so often seen through memory rather than today's life . . . these themes have always intrigued me, especially as they relate to identity."[2]

Halaby complicates notions of home through Hala, though. Just as Hala is described as returning "home" to Jordan from America at the start of the novel, she also describes herself as a visitor. (The Palestine she has never been to is also "home" to her.) More important, she chooses to leave Sharif's promise of marriage in order to go back to the United States, a decision she describes in comfortable, if not effusive, terms: "It is time to start something new, and something old, not to fix something unfinished" (204). Her return to Arizona, where she suddenly has no tolerance for her uncle Hamdi and aunt Fay's fancy but sterile home, denotes a philosophical and emotional acceptance of movement and ambiguity. Hala has made a decision that challenges the strictures of the American dream and the expectations of her Middle Eastern family.

In Hala's reaction to Hamdi and Fay's home, Halaby includes an interesting twist on Hala's decision to return to the United States. Here issues of ethnicity in the United States interact with issues of class, an appropriate move on Halaby's part given that the two are deeply connected. By expressing contempt for Hamdi and Fay's "no imagination house," Hala associates it with white ethnicity by contrasting it with what she perceives to be the liveliness of homes in the Arab world. "Funny how this never bothered me before," she observes (216). This newfound recognition means that Hala has integrated her connection to the Middle East with her awareness of the limitations of the United States as symbolized by Hamdi and Fay's design scheme. Of course, her epiphany relies on a particular conflation of class and proper American-ness that is just as reductive as the conflation of whiteness and proper American-ness. In other words, what Hala imagines to be quintessentially "American," coded as quintessentially "white American," exists in a specific upper-class space that excludes poor and working-class Americans, white or otherwise. Halaby thus highlights the mythology of normative American-ness as being rooted in class prejudice in addition to ethnocentrism.

Race and class are present throughout *West of the Jordan*, but it would probably be negligent to ignore the presence of gender as one of its social themes. The most conspicuous item of gender analysis is the novel's exclusively female narration, one that emphasizes a diversity of viewpoints, aspirations, and living situations among Arab Muslim women in the United States and the Middle East. There are no stock subservient women in *West of the Jordan*. There are no superhuman clichés, either. Halaby deploys realistic women whose power is expressed in both subtle and explicit ways, such as the strength of Hala's mother, Soraya's fierce independence, and Mawal's meticulous care for the past and future of Palestine.

Once in a Promised Land

Halaby's second novel, *Once in a Promised Land,* is very much a topical reflection. That is to say, the novel reflects on many of the most important topics of our day. Those topics revolve in some way around the events of September 11, 2001, and their numerous effects on American society and foreign policy. *Once in a Promised Land* reexamines some of the themes of *West of the Jordan* but is more focused on racism, state power, and the post–September 11 crackdown on civil liberties in the United States. In particular, the novel explores how anti-Arab racism and Islamophobia intersect with domestic policy and spill over into the way Americans deal with one another. I take a look at these themes in conjunction with Halaby's aesthetic framework.

Like the title *West of the Jordan,* the title *Once in a Promised Land* is a double entendre. The word *once* can denote a singular moment or a past era, or it can denote a sequence, as in "Once I arrived in the United States." The novel focuses on Jassim and Salwa Haddad, a married couple in Tucson, Arizona, each originally from Jordan and both of Palestinian origin. It is a linear tale that makes little use of unorthodox aesthetics, instead presenting a singular narrative with intermittent flashbacks and some deviations into storytelling. In many novels, Arab American and otherwise, political events contextualize characters' development. In *Once in a Promised Land,* this is not the case: political events directly affect the characters' development. In fact, I would argue that topical politics play a central role in the story's ability to function.

I do not view this authorial choice as a strike against the novel. I believe that Halaby provides readers with an important look at how constrictive life for Arab Americans can be since the events of September 11. To be sure, Jassim and Salwa are motivated by forces and issues that go beyond government surveillance and anti-Arab racism, but US domestic politics also force them into particular situations that they would otherwise have eschewed. Jassim, for instance, loses his job because of an FBI investigation—a case of political forces determining his personal situation.

Much of the novel revolves around those political forces, primarily the rise of suspicion toward those deemed to be Arab or Muslim in the aftermath of

September 11. After the attack, Jassim and Salwa's lives are immediately impacted, although Jassim is loath to accept their new reality. That impact is revealed when they are shopping in a department store shortly after September 11, and a young sales clerk named Amber calls security on Jassim, a move that infuriates Salwa, but that Jassim treats with deliberate equanimity. A visibly furious Salwa accosts Amber and demands to know why she called security. A shamed and confused Amber explains to her supervisor, Mandy, "You told us to report anything suspicious, and I thought he looked suspicious."[3] This explanation does not satisfy Salwa, who reluctantly accepts a disingenuous apology from Mandy and appears pleased to have adequately scolded Amber.

Halaby illuminates a variety of important political themes in this scene. Amber is guilty of racial stereotyping, but she is merely responding to the definitions of "suspicion" to which she has been subjected, a process in which her supervisor Mandy is complicit. By telling her employees to report anything suspicious, Mandy is practically assuring that a situation like Jassim's will arise, given that the predominant definition of *suspicious* is coterminous with Middle Eastern ethnicity. Amber therefore did something wrong morally, but she did not do anything wrong according to the ethos of post–September 11 fear in the United States. By highlighting Amber's naïveté, Halaby casts light on the broader society in which Amber is merely a tiny participant. Readers are led to understand that Mandy, despite her apparent contrition, is guiltier than Amber. The guiltiest party, however, is the collection of media and politicians who have worked hard to make certain that imagined Middle Eastern features are perceived as inherently threatening and thus worthy of suspicion.

This phenomenon, which occupies an important position in *Once in a Promised Land,* reflects what in previous critical work I have referred to as "imperative patriotism," a type of patriotic outlook in the post–September 11 United States that demands acquiescence to a particular notion of safety and the national interest. Imperative patriotism relies on a certain ethnic imagery to produce a distinction between "us" and "them," with "us" representing good Americans and "them" representing evildoers. Stereotypical imagery of the Middle Eastern male—beard, dark skin, menacing eyes, and so forth—accompanies representations of "them." Americans such as Jassim who are unfortunate enough to resemble that image automatically become threatening. Amber acts on the threat she imagines Jassim to embody by outing him as "suspicious." She therefore signifies a particular prejudice that exists in American society.

All of these issues arise from differences in the meaning of "America." As in *West of the Jordan*, "America" means numerous things in *Once in a Promised Land*, depending on the character or situation. To Salwa, whose cynicism grows in response to the indignities she faces as an Arab in the United States, America is an unattainable promise: "Only the America that pulled at her was not the America of her birth, it was the exported America of Disneyland and hamburgers, Hollywood and the Marlboro man, and therefore impossible to find" (49). It is for this reason that Salwa feels a nagging discomfort at her boss Joan's ostensibly compassionate suggestion that she hang an American flag decal from her car's back windshield: "You never know what people are thinking, and having this will let them know where you stand" (55). Halaby renders the suggestion ostensible—appearing to be true or sincere—by pointing to a notion of "America" that Joan assumes is universal, one that requires devotion to a certain type of patriotism exemplified (or demonstrated) by the American flag (another example of imperative patriotism).

Hanging the American flag on one's car in the week following the events of September 11 might mean many things: solidarity with the victims of the attacks; a token of mourning; support for the government; a metaphorical blank check for the use of military action. But no matter what their inspiration, most of those who hung flags assumed that a particular meaning would be transmitted and understood. Joan is operating from this assumption. Her concern for Salwa is genuine, and her desire to assure that Salwa remains safe is unassailable; the problem exists in her implicit demand that Salwa display a certain level of patriotic devotion with which Salwa is uncomfortable. "This will let them know where you stand" can be interpreted as an injunction just as easily as it can be understood as a suggestion.

Jassim fluctuates between these different conceptions of America. He tries to be reasonable as an antidote to what he perceives to be Salwa's political rigidity, but his pragmatism finally wears down as an FBI investigation results in the loss of his job and his faith in the system. Halaby pulls no punches here. Even Jassim's greatest advocate—his progressive, anti-Republican, antiwar boss, Marcus—has doubts about Jassim's humanity. While Marcus is complaining about the abuse of

Jassim's civil liberties to his wife, Ella, his implicit suspicion is activated. "Do you think [Jassim] could do something?" (236), Ella asks, "something" meaning an act of terrorism, in particular the poisoning of Tucson's water supply, which Jassim can access (but cannot, as Jassim explains repeatedly, breach in such a way). Although Marcus answers, "Are you kidding, Ella? You know Jassim. Why would you suggest that?" he silently acknowledges, "Not for the first time, his wife had brought to the surface the very thing that was nagging at him, harvested that vague doubt that had been lodged way back in his brain, undercutting the faith he had in others" (237). When times get tough, Jassim, it seems, will never fully escape the limitations of his ethnicity in the United States.

Once in a Promised Land in total is fundamentally about the limitations of ethnicity—more specifically, the limitations of using ethnicity as an indicator of behavior and as a way of organizing American society. September 11 assumes a type of primacy in this context; Halaby illustrates how the events of that day did not evoke complete unity but in many ways created division and distrust. The division and distrust end up playing themselves out on the bodies of Jassim and Salwa. Both characters become disconnected from one another in roughly the same proportion that they become disconnected from their society. Jassim appears to be holding things together until he accidentally hits a teenager with his Mercedes; the teenager dies at the scene, though Jassim is cleared of wrongdoing by the police. After the accident, Jassim's cherished routine is disrupted, and he finds himself taking comfort in the presence of a Denny's waitress named Penny. Salwa's disconnection is activated primarily by a pregnancy she hides from Jassim and a subsequent miscarriage, although Halaby makes it clear that Salwa has never felt as fully committed to the United States as Jassim, nor has she been entirely committed to their marriage as much as to the idea of their marriage. Shortly after her miscarriage, she finds herself involved in a seemingly inexplicable affair with Jake, a part-time teller at the bank and (unbeknownst to Salwa) a low-level drug dealer.

It might first appear to readers that Jassim and Salwa's behavior is counterintuitive, but in the framework of the events to which they are responding there is a certain logic that reveals a correlation between their inability to find comfort in a supposedly storybook life and American society's inability to fulfill its own dreams and ideals. Let us take a look at these four characters—Jassim, Salwa, Penny, and Jake—more closely to see how this correlation functions.

Jassim and Penny are remarkably different in terms of ethnicity, religion, class, and experience. Their differences are exemplified by a joint trip they make to Wal-Mart, where Jassim observes to himself, "In one breath he was in the souq in Amman, a place he couldn't stand, for the same reason he wouldn't have liked Wal-Mart if he hadn't been invited to go with Penny: too many poor people, too many products to sift through, all of questionable quality" (278). Jassim's classist outlook, which he hides from Penny, is counterbalanced by Penny's racist attitude, which she hides from Jassim. She tells her friend Trini, "He's from Jordan, but he's so different from those people," and "He's got a conscience. He's not some religious freak like them" (281). Jassim's innate attraction to Penny, then, arises from a certain feeling of alienation that he imagines Penny can satisfy. Penny's attraction to Jassim arises from the same hope, though she indicates that she is interested mainly in the lifestyle that Jassim's income might provide. The disconnect between America and "America" enacts itself in Jassim's consciousness, compelling him to engage in behavior that is normally out of character.

Salwa's foray into this type of ambiguity is even more shocking, if only for the fact that her behavior results in some steamy sexual encounters. When Salwa, a part-time real estate agent, learns that Jake has been bragging about their sexual encounters, one of which was a tryst at a client's well-appointed house, she develops the strength to leave him and decides to get herself together in Jordan. After her final good-bye to an intoxicated Jake, she finds herself being beaten on the head with a sharp-edged picture frame as she leaves his apartment. Salwa and Jassim's stories end as a pummeled Salwa lies in a hospital bed, though the novel continues with a brief "After." Jake's psychotic behavior, apparently activated by his drug use, begins with a verbal rather than a physical attack, as when he comments, "So you're running back to the pigsty?" (320). "The pigsty" refers to Jordan, a space that Salwa, like Jassim, can never fully escape, a reality indicated by Jake's choice of slur as he hits her: "Goddamn fucking Arab bitch!" (322). Her ethnicity is built into Americans' perception of her, and any negative associations with that ethnicity come forward in unguarded moments.

The most interesting aspect of her relationship with Jake is that she imagines Jake's white ethnicity to embody "America"; Jake thus represents a complete departure from Jassim. The comfort Salwa seeks in Jake, though, becomes violent, a reflection of much Arab and American interaction following September 11. While all of this is happening, Salwa's former love interest in Jordan, Hassan, unaware of her condition, leaves her a voicemail explaining that he has just been married and does not intend to contact her again. Hassan has terrible timing. He was in love with Salwa before she met Jassim, and many years later he attempts to contact her before he continues with his engagement. He is unsuccessful one time because she is in the middle of a miscarriage and another time because she is having sex with Jake. By the time she is planning on returning to Jordan, however, she is thinking fondly of Hassan, and it becomes clear that Hassan is the anti-Jake, the embodiment of the Middle East to her. Her incapacitation, then, is the physical articulation of her liminality.

The "After" section encapsulates this liminality. An unnamed storyteller and an unnamed listener converse in this section, as they do in a "Before" in which they urge readers to set aside their stereotypes of Arabs and Muslims. Reminiscent of Rabih Alameddine's structural aesthetics in *The Hakawati*, these sections frame the novel's moral issues through story. The "After" tells "a story old as life," of a man named Hassan who accidentally stabs his beloved maiden. An unnamed nightingale finally whisks the maiden away in the hope that she will recover from her wounds. The story collapses binaries with its various "yes and no" propositions and particularly in its abrupt ending, where the following exchange takes place between the teller and listener:

> *The end?*
> The end.
> *Wait a sec.*
> What is it?
> *There's no "they lived happily ever after"?*
> "Happily ever after" only happens in American fairy tales.
> *Wasn't this an American fairy tale?*
> It was and it wasn't. (335)

The story's ultimate ambiguity reflects the ambiguity of Salwa and Jassim's situations as their stories end. All of the stories reflect a certain social and political ambiguity that cannot be resolved through simplistic formulas and happy conclusions.

If one of Halaby's imperatives was to create a fluid narrative, then her choice of water as the novel's primary symbol is appropriate. When Jassim was a child, his uncle told him, "Water is what will decide things, not just for us but for every citizen of the world as well" (40). From this point forward, Jassim is fascinated with water. His interest extends beyond its physical properties to include its emotional and cultural resonance. His desire to see water as a resource that is better understood politically and his admiration of it as an awesome life force intimate a struggle to live responsibly and to engender sustainability. It is water that has created his stable life, but it is water's potential to overwhelm humans that has unraveled that life. Jassim understands that water needs to be respected and harnessed responsibly because it can create death as easily as it sustains life.

Halaby contextualizes this definition with American politics after September 11. It is not entirely unsurprising that Jassim's difficulties with federal officials begin while he is taking a shower. And it is after his daily swim—yet another encounter with water—that Jassim meets Jack Franks, a stranger who it turns out is a former marine with a zealous sense of patriotic duty. Jassim is immediately uncomfortable with Jack's seemingly innocuous but incessant questioning while they shower in separate stalls in the gymnasium locker room. Jack acts as a citizen spy for the local FBI office, loosely monitoring Jassim using a laughably amateur investigative method and then embellishing his findings in conversations with FBI agents. Jack dies suddenly of a heart attack, but his zeal has already caused Jassim and Salwa permanent damage.

In his most obvious incarnation, Jack Franks symbolizes a type of political culture following September 11 that Halaby clearly finds unappealing: the conflation of (imagined or real) Arab ethnicity with danger and the subsequent need purportedly to protect America by monitoring Arabs. Jack personifies the dangers of patriotism, especially when it becomes synonymous, as it often does, with notions of ethnic superiority. Less obvious, however, is Halaby's comment on the traditional representation of the Arab or Muslim male as a threat to the (white and Christian) American woman. A plethora of American films and books have used this theme, most famously the Sally Field movie *Not Without My Daughter*, about an Iranian American man married to a white American woman. The man is decent until he takes a visit to Iran with his wife and their daughter, at which point he suddenly becomes a sexist and religious extremist from whom Field must rescue their captive daughter.

In *Once in a Promised Land*, the story is less incendiary but no less meaningful politically. Jack's daughter, Cinda, he explains to Salwa, met a man from Jordan: "They got into drugs. Cinda was no angel, so it's hard to tell who started it. She ran off with him. I went all over the place trying to find them, even flew to Jordan and went to his godforsaken village. Never found them, but did travel around your country looking, and it was very beautiful. The people were very kind to me, as much as I wanted to hate every last one. I brought my kids up to be honest people. I don't know what happened to Cinda, where I failed her. The worst is not knowing what really happened" (34). Jack's daughter has "gone native," a phrase that negatively describes the process by which a civilized human immerses himself or herself in an supposedly uncivilized culture. Jack's openness with Salwa, a stranger, reveals a hurt and a vulnerability, but at the same time his underlying displeasure with Arab culture is evident. He avenges the loss of his daughter through a fulfillment of patriotic duty. In so doing, he conflates his daughter's body with America's body politic. Halaby thus inverts the typical conflation of Arab women's bodies with Middle Eastern politics by showing the lapsed American (Jack's daughter) to be synonymous with a loss of national identity.

Although *Once in a Promised Land* is topical—rooted in a particular time and place—its themes go beyond the mainstreaming of anti-Arab racism and the erosion of civil liberties in the United States after September 11. In presenting those themes, Halaby also comments on the expansion of state power when a crisis unfolds; the activation of human distrust based on categories of ethnicity and religion; and the disparity between mythologies of immigration and its difficult realities. Although *Once in a Promised Land* will certainly be known as a novel that captures the anxieties of a particular moment in American history, it also entails a universal character study of the desires and flaws of humankind.

Conclusion

In his introduction to the Arab American poetry anthology *Inclined to Speak*, poet and critic Hayan Charara argues, "Regrettably, many Americans still register the complaint that since the [September 11] attacks, Arabs, Muslims, Arab Americans, and Muslim Americans have not spoken out enough about violence and terrorism. Most regrettable is the fact that this presumption is simply false. They have spoken out, and they have done so regularly, loudly, and in great numbers."[4] Charara goes on to explain that all the poets represented in his anthology have dealt in some way with issues of violence, an observation that is true of Arab American fiction writers. Halaby is among the handful of fiction writers who deal with issues of violence directly as well as allegorically. Both *West of the Jordan* and *Once in a Promised Land* examine not only the violence of terrorism (Eastern and Western), but also the violence that exists in racism, assimilation, and domestic policy. Halaby does not confine violence to the realm of the physical. She instead shows it to be something that is interconnected across the spectra of war, politics, culture, and everyday life.

7

Crescent Moons, Jazz Music, and Feral Ethnicity

Diana Abu-Jaber

DIANA ABU-JABER is one of the preeminent Arab American writers today. Her first novel, *Arabian Jazz* (1993), was the first work of modern Arab American fiction to reach a wide critical and commercial audience. She has subsequently built on her early success with *Crescent* and *Origin* as well as with a memoir, *The Language of Baklava,* all best-sellers. Accompanying Abu-Jaber's success is much lively discussion among Arab American literary critics about the merits of and problems in her work. This discussion takes place because Abu-Jaber employs a distinct ethnic presence in her writing, which is evident in the way her work is packaged and promoted. In many ways, she is at the nexus of the category "Arab American literature" because her work impels critics to examine not only the uses of ethnic imagery in the category, but the very parameters of the category itself.

It is likely that Abu-Jaber is aware of this position. Not all of her works deal explicitly with Arab Americans. *Origin,* for instance, does not even mention Arabs or Arab Americans, an omission that suggests Abu-Jaber wanted to shake up the conversation about the content and range of Arab American writing. Let us take a look at each of her three novels in the order in which they were published.

Arabian Jazz

Arabian Jazz was the first Arab American novel published since Etel Adnan's *Sitt Marie Rose* had appeared more than a decade earlier. (Joseph Geha's *Through and Through* was published before *Arabian Jazz,* but it is a short story collection.) It would help generate an interest in Arab American fiction that eventually led to the steady publication of Arab American novels throughout the 1990s, which has in turn developed into today's prolific and diverse fiction.

In a profile of Abu-Jaber, Alice Evans points out that *Arabian Jazz* "is thought to be the first novel published about the Arab-American experience."[1] Although the first novel about the Arab American experience might be difficult to identify—especially given the myriad criteria for a novel's composition—it is inaccurate to bestow this accolade on *Arabian Jazz.* The ethnic continuity between the Arab world and Arab America clouds attempts at compartmentalizing this literature into specific periods. Even more to the point, Kahlil Gibran and Ameen Rihani, members of al-Muhjar (the immigrants), wrote novels while in the United States during the first half of the twentieth century, Etel Adnan published *Sitt Marie Rose* in 1977, and Elmaz Abinader's *Children of the Roojme,* defined at times as a novel and others as an autobiography, appeared in 1991. Nonetheless, Abu-Jaber is a seminal figure in the Arab American literary tradition. The publication of *Arabian Jazz* signaled a much broader way of approaching and constructing fictional accounts of Arab American society and as a result set much higher stakes for those Arab Americans who would write after it was published.

The novel, set in 1990, focuses on the Ramoud family in Euclid, New York, thirty miles outside of Syracuse. The main characters are Matussem Ramoud, his daughters Melvina (Melvie) and Jemorah (Jem), and his older sister, Fatima Mawadi. Their personalities are a study in contrasts. Free-spirited Matussem is an easy-going jazz drummer when he is not occupied by his maintenance job at the hospital. Twenty-two-year-old Melvina, eight years younger than Jemorah, is remarkably serious, driven fanatically by her duties as the hospital's head nurse. Jemorah is Melvina's opposite, meandering along without focus as a hospital filing clerk. And Fatima, whose goal is to marry off her nieces at any cost, is ceaselessly overbearing, more concerned with social appearance than with emotional reality. Jemorah and Melvina's mother, Nora, an Irish American, died of tuberculosis during a visit to Jordan when Jemorah was nine. As a remembered figure, she acts as both a stabilizing force and a source of conflict. Nora's parents blamed Matussem for her death, barely disguising their belief that his being Arab had much to do with it, and Matussem's relatives never fully accepted Nora into the familial unit. It is in large part because of her memory that the Ramouds slowly grow closer. These characters stumble through the narrative, at times in burlesque fashion, toward a better understanding of themselves and their world.

The novel's most striking attribute may be its humor. Humor, Abu-Jaber believes, can improve a story's reception: "I thought it would be a fairly serious book at first, actually, but humor seemed to present itself as a natural medium— I suppose because when you're not sure what sort of reception your story will have, humor seems to offer more accessibility or intimacy."[2] "Take for example Uncle Fouad," Evans writes, "who, while visiting from Jordan, parades around in various stages of undress, finally wearing only a facecloth to cup his genitals."[3] In another scene at a church-sponsored dinner for a visiting Jordanian archbishop, a brawl ensues in which "everyone was shouting in Arabic, shrieking about mothers, Arabs, Americans, and patriotism in general. From what Jem could tell, the men—though all drunk—swiftly factionalized, Saudis with Saudis, Lebanese with Lebanese, and so on. There was civil war at the back of the St. Yusef Syrian Orthodox Church."[4] Earlier at the dinner, Aunt Fatima tried to set Jem up with "an old-looking young man named Salaam Alaikum [an Islamic greeting meaning 'peace be upon you']. His face was so thick with sorrow it seemed to hang in the folds of the skin. His eyes appeared to be liquid, about to leak into the seams of his cheeks" (63). Toward the end of the book, Matussem, whose family is Syrian Orthodox, climbs onto his roof early one Saturday morning to conduct Muslim prayers, yelling at his daughter, "Melvina, you're a heartpicker, you heartpicker" (355).

Literary critics throughout the years have suggested that in fiction humor can operate in both meditative and reflexive fashion. This is clearly the case with *Arabian Jazz*. The technique of humor lessens the strain on Abu-Jaber to translate cultural difference into commonplace, stereotypical terms. She employs it to suggest how cultural duality and human conflict are negotiated, resolved, and renegotiated in everyday life.

In *Arabian Jazz*, Abu-Jaber deliberately crosses cultural boundaries in order to situate the concerns of Arab Americans into a more generally comprehensible framework. "I was searching for a long time for a metaphor for Palestinians that Americans could grasp in a visceral way," she explained to Evans in 1996. "This country can tend to be so isolated and so muffled from what's happening outside of its borders." She gradually realized that "the experiences of Native Americans were so similar to what was happening to Palestinians, the way they were slowly phased out or pushed back, how there were moments of violence, but that native peoples were always constituted as savages or barbarians."[5] This recognition becomes integral to *Arabian Jazz* when Jemorah and Ricky Ellis, a half-Onondaga gas station attendant, become lovers. Both have been made marginal by their community and first found solace in one another as children, without conversation. Although they never solidify a relationship, their intercourse symbolizes the entrance of one ethnic movement into the fold of another. The intercommunication provides comfort amid surroundings where Arab and Indian are often represented as being subhuman; their relationship thus serves as a sentimental counterpoint to the humorous negotiations in the novel.

In *Arabian Jazz*, contextualizing the Arab within a broader rubric of minority discourse produces a textual paradox worth our attention: Abu-Jaber creates an essentialized Other—the Arab American—who interacts with other marginalized characters so that the essentialist tendencies of the dominant society can be mitigated and ultimately restructured. This move is more than strategic essentialism, however. ("Strategic essentialism," a concept developed by the theorist Gayatri Chakravorty Spivak, refers to the ways that individuals or communities use essentialism—the reduction of groups of people to essences—to their advantage.) Rather, it expands on strategic essentialism to underscore a doubling of identity—Arab/American—that is ultimately negotiated into a modern ethnic community—Arab America—through aesthetic markers such as humor, irony, and pastiche as well as through dialogue with non-Arab double Others.

A contrast to Jemorah and Ricky is Jemorah's supervisor, Portia Porshman. Throughout the novel, the hospital where Jemorah works acts metaphorically as an imprisoning social environment for her. She has tried numerous times to quit but has hopelessly bent under Portia's intimidation, noting each time that the entire clerical staff seems eternally bound to the machinery of the office controlled by Portia. Jemorah, recalling that she had recently decided to quit for good, considers her constant hesitation: "Wednesday morning pressed down on Jem. She felt the eternal recurrence of work that was continually undoing itself; she could hardly bear another day, losing her life hour by hour. The team leader had talked her into staying on until they could find her replacement. Two weeks' notice turned into a summer, and perhaps longer: they hadn't even advertised the opening yet. She went to work thinking, This is absolutely my last week" (289).

Yet in the end it is Portia who drives Jemorah from the hospital. In the novel's gravest scene, Portia calls Jemorah into her office and embarks on a diatribe naively intended to keep Jemorah under her command. The rant is worth quoting in full:

> Your mother used to be such a good, good girl. She was so beautifully white, pale as a flower. And then, I don't know. What happened? The silly girl wanted attention. She met your father in her second year [of college] and she just wanted attention. We just weren't enough for her. I'll tell you, we couldn't believe it. This *man*, he couldn't speak a word of our language, didn't have a real job. And Nora was so—like a flower, a real flower, I'm telling you. It seemed like three days after she met that man they were getting married. A split second later she was pregnant. I know for a fact her poor mother—your grandmother—had to ask for a picture of the man for her parish priest to show around to prove he wasn't a Negro. Though he might as well have been, really, who could tell the difference, the one lives about the same as the other. (293–94)

The scene culminates with the hospital office transformed from a metaphor of totalitarian control into an arena of forced assimilation:

> She never did finish college after that, never got to be the woman she could've been. A husband and baby at twenty. Look at what *I've* done with my life. You know, it's not too late for you. Oh, sure, you're tainted, your skin that color. A damn shame. But I've noticed that in certain lights it's worse than in others. Your mother could have made such beautiful children—they could have been so lovely, like she was, like a white rose. Still, it could definitely have been worse for you, what with *his* skin. Now, if you were to change your name, make it Italian maybe, or even Greek, that might help some. I'm telling you this for love of your mother. I'll feel forever I might have saved her when that Arab man took her and you kids back to that horrible country of his over there [Jordan]. It's a wonder any of you survived that place, so evil, primitive, filled with disease! I should've spoken up twenty years ago, but I didn't. I thought, the Lord will provide, blah, blah. . . . I'm telling you, Jemorah Ramoud, your father and all his kind aren't any better than Negroes, that's why he hasn't got any ambition and why he'll be stuck in that same job in the basement for the rest of his life. . . . We'll try putting some pink lipstick on you, maybe lightening your hair, make you *American*. (294)

The statements in this speech are direct and candid. It seems that when contemplating this aspect of America, Abu-Jaber has no use for subtlety. It is a situation that has precedent in her own childhood: "Abu-Jaber explains," states Evans, that "even though Syracuse had a large Arab-American community, even though she and her two sisters were surrounded by uncles, aunts, and cousins who lived in or visited the community, even though they were encouraged to identify with their Arab heritage, they were told by their Jordanian-American relatives to stay out of the sun to protect their milky white complexions so they could pass as white Americans."[6]

Abu-Jaber's aunts and cousins made a decision that is bound to be controversial among both white and minority Americans. It would be perfectly appropriate for us to debate the wisdom of such advice, but it might be more useful at this point to acknowledge that the reason for its existence in the first place is attitudes like Portia's. Of note is the fact that until her outburst, her racism is tacit, so Jemorah is not aware of it even as it is affecting her career. Like characters we have encountered in the work of Laila Halaby and Susan Muaddi Darraj, Portia conflates proper American-ness with whiteness, an attitude that is common enough for Abu-Jaber's elders to have urged her to emphasize her white appearance. As we have seen, when this sort of conflation occurs, a rigid sense of identity becomes codified. In *Arabian Jazz*, Abu-Jaber illuminates how identity can be codified but simultaneously writes enough complexity into her Arab American characters that such boundaries are immediately crossed.

Crescent

In her two novels after *Arabian Jazz*, Abu-Jaber moves away from explicit political themes. Her writing entails a more subtle presentation of social and cultural issues. *Crescent* covers many of the same themes evident in *Arabian Jazz*, but the two books are decidedly different. (The gap of time—ten years—between the novels is itself indicative of the author's development.) *Arabian Jazz* is a comic novel, one that sacrifices narrative cohesion for playful upheaval, but one that is also deadly serious in many of its themes, including anti-Arab racism and the purported infanticide of Palestinian children (an inclusion for which Abu-Jaber has been criticized because there is no historical evidence to show that Palestinians ever committed infanticide, even after their dispossession). *Crescent*, in contrast, deals with a host of concerns in the Arab American community, but it uses a poetic structure that departs significantly from *Arabian Jazz*.

Crescent might best be described as a study in character. That is to say, the novel is driven more by an intimate exploration of character than it is by a fast-moving plot. Taking place in "Tehrangeles," a Los Angeles neighborhood inhabited by a large population of Iranians and other Middle Easterners, *Crescent* is narrated through the point of view of Sirine, a thirty-nine-year-old Iraqi American who lives with her uncle, a UCLA professor. Sirine is a chef at a local Arabic restaurant, Nadia's Café, run by Um-Nadia (mother of Nadia), a strong-willed person anchored in the Middle Eastern community of Los Angeles. Sirine eventually falls in love with Hanif El-Eyad (Han), an Iraqi expatriate who joins the UCLA faculty as a linguist. A diverse collection of patrons—including Lon Hayden, head of the Near Eastern Studies Department—frequents Nadia's Café. These patrons create a multinational and multicultural interaction, rendering the café a quintessentially international space.

According to the literary critic Carol Fadda-Conrey, Nadia's Café serves to broaden perceptions of what *Arab* means, transforming the term from a narrow descriptor to a sundry referent:

> Even though most of the Arab cafe regulars remain in the novel's background and do not play an active role in the plot, the careful delineation of their individual national differences negates simplistic representations of Arab identity. The names of the Arab students from Egypt and Kuwait—Schmaal, Jenoob, Shark, and Gharb, which in Arabic mean North, South, East, and West, respectively—signify distinct geographical entities that can be interpreted as individualized characteristics challenging the reductive attributes the term Arab often generates."[7]

As in *Arabian Jazz*, Abu-Jaber is concerned with Arab American ethnicity in *Crescent*, but her presentation of the issue is more subtle and symbolic. Throughout the novel, Nadia's Café serves as a worldly space despite its modest physical size. It allows Arab voices to move beyond restricted forms of articulation.

This focus on border crossing is an integral theme in *Crescent*. In Nadia's Café, for instance, the interchange among the patrons happens within a new set of rules, those that informally govern the café in place of the rules of a state or a specific culture. It is in Nadia's Café that Sirine helps orient the internationals in American life: "For many of [the Arab students] the café was a little flavor of home."[8] Nadia's Café encapsulates many of these themes of distance and loneliness, perhaps not entirely by chance. Sirine notes that "Um-Nadia says the loneliness of the Arab is a terrible thing; it is all-consuming. It is already present like a little shadow under the heart when he lays his head on his mother's lap; it threatens to swallow him whole when he leaves his own country, even though he marries and travels and talks to friends twenty-four hours a day" (9). Although Um-Nadia's observation might be taken as poetic or hyperbolic, depending on the individual reader's viewpoint, it brings into focus a main theme of the novel—continual placelessness.

The sense of placelessness that Um-Nadia identifies permeates *Crescent*, starting with Sirine, who adheres to a routine but nevertheless is given to loneliness or feelings of being uprooted. She eventually finds an expression of her feelings through Han, who explains to her, "The fact of exile is bigger than everything else in my life" (162). By describing exile as a "fact," Han suggests that it is immutable, something that not only influences his life but plays a central role in defining it. It is a feeling that Sirine understands. Han continues, "Leaving my country was like—I don't know—like part of my body was torn away. I have phantom pains from the loss of that part—I'm haunted by myself." "I think I can get it," Nadia responds (162). In Abu-Jaber's usage, the term *exile* means more than separation from home. It is a condition. The condition of exile transcends physical movement. Sirine lives in the city in which she was born, and yet she shares (or at least understands) the exile's pain, in this case Han's. Much of *Crescent* explores what it means to create a sense of place in exile.

Nadia's Café also provides *Crescent* with another important motif: food. Many Arab American writers have used food motifs, as have authors from other ethnic backgrounds. One of the seminal early Arab American texts, for example, is a poetry anthology entitled *Grape Leaves*, and it was followed by titles such as *Food for Our Grandmothers* and Abu-Jaber's memoir *The Language of Baklava*. In that memoir, Abu-Jaber uses baklava—the Greek/Middle Eastern fillo and walnut pastry—as a symbolic food item into which culture and language can be inscribed. Or, put more simply, baklava is an expression of Arab culture and the language Arabs use to make that culture come to life. Abu-Jaber's symbolic use of baklava is similar to Muaddi Darraj's use of such motifs, though Muaddi Darraj is less heavy-handed in her presentation of culture through food.

In *Crescent*, the use of food as a cultural motif is subtle, but it comprises one of the novel's primary poetic devices. Sirine relishes the opportunity she has to work with food and create new dishes, which allows her to express her creativity and engage a community of diners. The food she cooks brings people together and provides her with her livelihood. When she cooks for Han, "The aroma of garlic, grilled lamb, and open fields fills the kitchen. She brings it to the table on a big plate with rice cooked with saffron and toasted pine nuts. She tries to eat a little of it herself, but the meat is tasteless; she can barely swallow it. So instead she sits and watches Han eat, hoping, in this simple act, to draw him in" (290). Sirine's actions here are more complex than they may first seem. First of all, the description of the aromas of her food belies the description of it as tasteless, which means that its tastelessness is symbolic, in this case of Sirine's anxiety about her relationship with Han. More important, in conceptualizing eating as a "simple act," Sirine either downplays its profound importance or suggests that drawing Han in will be an act of simplicity. It can be a simple act only through the presence of the food she has created, which not only sustains life but improves its quality.

Another important motif in *Crescent* is the storytelling function assumed by Sirine's uncle, a bit of a mysterious character whose role in the narrative is crucial. Each chapter begins from his point of view, with his telling a story that is allegorically relevant to the novel's action. Abu-Jaber's inclusion of a storytelling uncle is important in a few ways. It recalls Rabih Alameddine's focus on the story as a profound element of Arab culture and history. It also bespeaks a communicative (and communal) tradition of oral authority and cultural sharing through the medium of story. Much modern Arab American writing, in all genres, includes the portrayal of storytellers, usually male, and often an uncle (such as Jihad in Alameddine's *The Hakawati*). Abu-Jaber frequently illuminates this tradition, particularly in *The Language of Baklava*.

Some of the issues raised in *Crescent* are less metaphysical and more oriented around topical politics. The longstanding American military presence in Iraq is a recurrent issue. The Iraqi characters are exiled because of Saddam Hussein's brutality or the instability of war in general. At times, Abu-Jaber is pointed in her criticism of American involvement in Iraq, referencing the crippling economic sanctions of the 1990s and the air-bombing campaigns that killed numerous civilians. She also takes on issues of racism in conjunction with her exploration of immigration and exile. One reason why Um-Nadia owns a restaurant is that she bought it from another Arab owner whose business declined when FBI agents frequented it in search of terrorists following the Gulf War. Um-Nadia immediately drove away the agents once she took over the space. At one point, Sirine recalls, "Sometimes she used to scan the room and imagine the word *terrorist*. But her gaze ran over the faces and all that came back to her were words like *lonely*, and *young*" (19).

Here Sirine is reconfiguring typical uses of language in the United States. *Terrorist* is a term generally used in conjunction with images of Arabs and Muslims, a fact that Sirine reinforces by looking at Arabs and Muslims and then automatically associating them with terrorists. After a moment of contemplation, however, she accesses the truth of their existence beyond the stereotypes that existence represents. In this way and others, Abu-Jaber seems interested in the way language communicates meaning. In a conversation with Han, Sirine wonders if Iraqi jokes and fables are like "secret codes," to which Han replies, "In America, you say 'secret code,' but in Iraq, that's just the way things are. Everything's sort of folded up and layered, just a bit more complicated" (46). This distinction indicates that life in Iraq is much more complicated than many Americans might imagine, and Iraqis' imaginative uses of language embody its complexity. Abu-Jaber attempts to reproduce this linguistic complexity throughout *Crescent* by folding up and layering her fictive language, producing a read that relies on the reader's imagination for full comprehensibility.

Abu-Jaber also makes it seem as if she was aware of the specific ways that cultural meanings are inscribed in language when she was writing *Crescent*. (It might be useful for me to point out that I do not believe that making an attempt to decode an author's intention is a very good way to critique literature. Such a technique, which literary critics refer to as "the intentional fallacy," usually does not work well for two main reasons: the reader is not a psychic and cannot possibly know what was in the author's mind when he or she wrote a work of literature; and the author's intent does not matter as much as what ultimately got written. In other words, even if an author intended for something to happen, that does not mean he or she actually accomplished that goal.) Abu-Jaber appears to be aware of these static cultural meanings because some elements of *Crescent* undermine them, an accomplishment that would be impossible without an awareness of them.

After Sirine has her public fallout with her friend Rana, for instance, they sit together and converse about their dislike for one another, which Rana attributes to Sirine's unfounded fear that Rana wants to be romantically involved with Han. Rana then begins telling Sirine about her arranged marriage to a wealthy second cousin, Fareed, who turned out to be abusive. At one point in her story, she stops herself and asks Sirine, "You want to hear all this? . . . I don't like to tell my American friends, it just feeds all the usual stereotypes—you know, the sheikh with the twenty virgins, all that stuff" (281). Rana's qualification recalls Soraya's tricksterism in *West of the Jordan* and Reema's ethnic burden in *The Inheritance of Exile*. When Sirine responds, "Don't worry, I won't think that," a certain meaning is coded within a seemingly simple sentence. Sirine invokes their ethnic affiliation without referring to it explicitly. Her ability to understand and thus not to judge Rana arises primarily from the intensity of the moment, but also from their shared ethnicity and the unspoken recognitions that accompany it.

This treatment of ethnicity is generally understated throughout *Crescent*, which makes it an aesthetically different novel than *Arabian Jazz*, which explores ethnicity explicitly, sometimes in parody. Either style has its advantage: *Arabian Jazz* uses humor through its parodies, but *Crescent* acquires a depth of character and philosophy that must exist for a novel to be considered artistically successful. *Origin*, as we shall see, presents yet another poetic departure for Abu-Jaber.

Origin

Abu-Jaber's third novel presents a number of interesting questions about modern Arab American fiction. It is an "Arab American" novel that appears to have no Arab characters. The sentence I just wrote in itself brings up some interesting points.

First, just because *Origin* does not appear to have any Arab characters does not mean that it actually contains none. It may well. Abu-Jaber does not tell readers whether any of the characters is Arab or not. For the most part, she avoids naming ethnicities in *Origin*, although she does describe features (which may confirm stereotypes or evoke speculation but cannot definitively name ethnic identity). The main exception is the character Keller Duseky, whose ethnicity further obfuscates rather than clarifies these matters: "My great-great grandparents [were Czeck]. . . . And Swiss, French, Irish."[9] Second, it is not entirely clear that *Origin* is an "Arab American" novel. (Of course, I would argue that it is unclear whether any novel is really "Arab American" or under what conditions a novel achieves such an identification.) Nothing about its content or its packaging (in the hardback edition) suggests that it is an "ethnic" novel. So I apparently have included the novel in this book based on my knowledge of its author's ethnic background or based on her status as a well-known Arab American author.

Third, by noting that the novel appears to have no Arab characters, I am reading those characters into the novel. If it were not for Abu-Jaber's reputation or the development of a category of "Arab American" literature, this move would have been highly unlikely.

For many years, literary critics, teachers, students, and reading groups have pondered what the world of books would be like if we did not divvy writing into ethnic categories. This speculation is difficult to entertain for long, though, because in order to picture such a world we would need to do away with other categories such as nationality and genre (poetry, essay, fiction, drama). Most important, we would need to get rid of the category "literature" itself, which is supposed to distinguish "good" or "proper" fiction and poetry from mere pop writing (e.g., Danielle Steele, Dean Koontz, James Patterson). It is basically impossible to have a system in which books are published selectively and sold on an open market without upholding a number of categories, even if the literature itself does not neatly conform to them.

Another interesting question is easier to entertain: What would an "ethnic" novel look like if it had no ethnic characters? (All humans, of course, have an ethnicity; by "ethnic characters," I mean the characters who are recognized to belong to an ethnic minority community, which is usually what the term connotes.) Here is where *Origin* deviates from the Arab American fiction that preceded it. By not identifying any of her characters as Arab, Abu-Jaber is making a specific political point in addition to an artistic choice. It is possible that she simply wanted to move away from being typecast as an ethnic author, but her choice not to name Arabs ultimately reinforces the importance of culture and identity in literature. Think of it as an inclusion by omission.

It is interesting that *Origin*, without identifiable Arab characters, would be considered a part of the Arab American literary tradition, especially considering that Abu-Jaber is not the only author of Arab background to deploy characters who are not visibly Arab. *The Exorcist* author, William Peter Blatty, for example, is of Lebanese background. The well-known writers Jane Brox and Mona Simpson are likewise of Arab origin. None of these writers is usually classified as "Arab American," mainly because they do not participate in that category and because they do not explore themes that are normally associated with Arabs and Arab Americans. Writers such as Abu-Jaber, however, do employ such themes and are marketed by their publishers as ethnic writers (which might pigeonhole them but also creates a market niche to sell books).

Despite the absence of ethnic characters, *Origin* nevertheless explores ethnicity. Protagonist Lena Dawson's colleague Margo, for instance, has children named Amahl and Fareed. There is no solid evidence to suggest that through these names the children are "ethnic," whatever that means (in the United States, it usually means "nonwhite"), but the names are Arabic in origin. A physical description of Margo and her children is absent from *Origin*. The same is true of Lena's neighbor, Mr. Memdouah, an eccentric character who plays a tacit role in unraveling the novel's central mystery. His name suggests an African or Muslim origin, but readers are never told whether that suggestion has any merit. In another case, even when Abu-Jaber focuses on a physical description, she still manages to make a character's origin ambiguous. Lena flashes back to the case of Troy Haverstraw, a boy who was murdered outside of Syracuse; Lena solved the crime, which earned her a reputation as an insightful investigator. Troy's parents are white, but he was actually fathered by a Mexican migrant worker. Abu-Jaber describes him as a "wheat-skinned boy" and as having "café au lait skin" (62). It turns out that Troy was murdered by his father, Jimmy, in part because of Jimmy's inability to come to grips with his son's unknown origin.

Troy's mother, Anita, "might've been part Iroquois or Oneida, possibly French or Spanish" (64). Needless to say, these ethnicities are highly disparate, so Abu-Jaber is purposefully casting a broad net around Anita's background, indicating that her ethnic origin (whatever it is) might not actually correspond with her ethnic identity (as generically white). One of the families in the novel goes by the name "Handal," a well-known Palestinian name, but, again, that does not necessarily make the Handals Palestinian. Lena, too, is described as having dark but vague features. Because she is an adopted child, her adoptive parents, Pia and Henry McWilliams, do not know exactly what her origin is, and her quest for knowledge of this sort comprises the novel's central theme. Very few characters in the novel are assigned a stable origin or identity. This move is both aesthetic and philosophical. It is aesthetic in the sense that a search for identity and rootedness is vital to the novel's meaning. It is philosophical in the sense that Abu-Jaber is playing around with the typical distinctions between "white" and "ethnic" by assigning "ethnic" signals to characters and situations that may well be perceived as "white" and vice versa. *Origin* is an ethnic novel by design, not by default.

Now I feel a bit guilty for focusing so heavily on sociologica. So let us get to other parts of the novel, shall we? I have established that one of the primary themes in *Origin* is identity and rootedness. This theme affects multiple characters but is most evident in Lena. Lena is on something of a quest, not simply to solve a series of crimes, but also to discover the mysterious elements of her own origin. She helps convince her higher-ups in a Syracuse forensics lab to reopen a case in which a baby's death was attributed to sudden infant death syndrome. Although she faces skepticism at first, it eventually becomes clear that Syracuse has a child serial killer on its hands. For reasons unknown to her, she feels profoundly drawn to the case, thinking that her past and present somehow play a role in the murders. She suspects that she needs to learn about her origin in order to solve the case.

Lena's suspicion proves correct. She is implicated tacitly in the case, and she can solve it only in conjunction with important discoveries about her own origin. She is resentful of Pia and Henry for never having formally adopted her, but it turns out that they acquired Lena as a toddler from an underground adoption service that operated outside of the system. The murderer, an elderly woman named Opal, is aware of this history. Having lost one of her own infants many years ago, Opal believes she is on a mission from God to save "damaged babies," those who "were born without souls" (354). The "damaged babies" of concern to Opal are like Lena, adopted through the rogue adoption agency run by Myrtle. All of the murdered infants were born to such mothers; Opal is intent on halting what she imagines to be their evil bloodlines. Throughout the novel, she secretly poisons Lena, whose death will be the final link in Opal's plan. Lena's death also ironically will be the missing link to her own past, something she is fortunately able to recognize while she is still alive.

Lena's story is more complex than her guerrilla adoption. Until the end of the novel, she believes that she was a feral child raised by gorillas somewhere in the tropics. Because Abu-Jaber avoids situational irony, readers are led to believe the same. (Situational irony happens when the audience is aware of something that one of the characters is not.) Lena conveys to readers the sense that there is much more to her story than we know, but her suspicion that she has special abilities because of her feral origin seems viable given her memories. In fact, her memories of a gorilla mother figure are only somewhat accurate. It turns out that she used to play with and cling to an oversized stuffed gorilla in Myrtle's house as a toddler. Lena's adoptive mother, Pia, cannot tell Lena about her real past because of Pia's fear that her illegal act will be uncovered. Lena is finally satisfied regarding her newfound knowledge of her origin and happy to learn that she was not a feral child. Her special investigative abilities are a result of simpler things: intuition and talent.

A political commentary is inscribed in these events. Lena appears to be happy with her discoveries, despite the fact that even though she has learned what she was not as a baby, she never finds out who she is. After reading a police report about being discovered in a dumpster when she was a baby, Lena realizes, "The beauty of reading a report on one's own origins is that it lets you walk away from everything—from history, obligations, connections. It's a new creation myth—perhaps just as disturbing as learning one was raised by apes in the rain forest. To be a baby thrown into the garbage is to be in a plane crash. And—whether I was rescued by a police officer or an ape—I was rescued" (378). Lena's realization allows her to proceed more comfortably with her life. She decides that knowing one's origin can be as cumbersome as not knowing it. Abu-Jaber couches these thoughts in the language of "creation myths," a way of suggesting that all humans need stories of their origins, and if they do not have one built in to their identities, then it becomes necessary to create one anew. Lena does this by visiting the dumpster into which she was deposited as a baby. She gets to invent her own origin myth because she never fully learns of the facts surrounding her abandonment. "Some stories—sometimes—shouldn't be told," an elderly Greek diner owner advises Lena (383).

Abu-Jaber employs a bit of heavy-handed symbolism around Lena's transformation. In particular, she alters the novel's ambiance at the end when Lena achieves a certain level of comfort. Throughout *Origin*, one of the main narrative techniques is Abu-Jaber's description of Syracuse and its severe winter, a seemingly endless onslaught of ice, snow, and wind. Syracuse and its climate become an important part of the story, not only because of the ambiance they create, but also because wintertime assists Lena in solving crimes (she can detect footprints, for example). Once the child murder crimes are solved, the weather begins to transition into springtime, when Lena, along with the flora and fauna of Syracuse, is renewed. This symbolism is not terribly different from the symbolism George Harrison had in mind when he wrote "Here Comes the Sun."

At the novel's close, Lena suggests that she is aware of the symbolic transformation proffered by weather: "When I was a child, I used to lose track of the transition from winter to spring. It seemed to me that one day there would be piles of snow and the next would be all green. Often, during a long winter, I rushed to the window in the morning hoping that the earth had transformed from its white panes of ice back to the sweet green world" (384). In leaving winter and entering into the sweet green world, Lena has lost something: the sharpness of her senses and her sensibilities that winter provides. The spring, in other words, would not be so sweet without the intensity of winter.

Conclusion

Abu-Jaber is a seminal figure in modern Arab American letters. With her status comes a bit of controversy, however. Some Arab American critics have criticized her for her portrayal of Palestinians and Arab American society. Although I do not want to speak on those controversies here (they are more appropriate for a different book), I will point out that the controversy she generates indicates first and foremost a high level of success. It is nearly impossible for a writer to represent any ethnic, national, or religious community without irritating somebody. That is simply the nature of representation and reading. Perhaps this is why Abu-Jaber chose to avoid explicit representation in *Origin*—to make a point about its inevitability without having to describe any community directly. In any case, it will be impossible for future literary historians to discuss Arab American literature without including Abu-Jaber; it is also just as likely that she will enter into any fruitful discussion of American literature without any hyphens.

8

From the Maghreb to the American Mainstream

Writers of North African Origin

(Anouar Majid, Laila Lalami, Samia Serageldin)

THE ARAB WORLD is broken into two broad regions: the Middle East, also known as the Near East, West Asia, and the Mashreq, which often is a synecdoche for the entire Arab world (a part representing the whole); and North Africa, also known as the Maghreb, which includes the Arab world's most populous country (Egypt), Africa's largest (the Sudan), former French colonies (Tunisia, Algeria, and Morocco), and a former Italian colony (Libya). These nations are often discussed as if they are part of the Middle East, even though Morocco is only a few miles from Spain. Speaking of the Middle East in this way is obviously a geopolitical rather than a strictly geographical identification, but North Africa has its own unique cultures, histories, and linguistic styles that separate it from the Asian Arab countries, although both African and Asian Arabs consider themselves to be ethnic brethren.

When it comes to Arab American literature, North Africa tends to be overlooked. Part of North Africa's marginality has to do with simple demographics: there are simply not as many American writers of North African background as there are of Near Eastern background. The Libyan Khaled Mattawa is a decorated poet, critic, and translator, but no other Libyan writer in the United States is nearly as prominent (Hisham Matar, another noted Libyan writer, lives in the United Kingdom). There are not many Tunisian American writers (the critic Nouri Gana comes to mind). Most of the works published by Algerian writers in the United States—a considerable number—were translated into English from French or Arabic. No Moroccan Americans have published novels in the United States besides Laila Lalami and Anouar Majid, both of whom I discuss in this chapter.

Near Eastern writers, in contrast, are overwhelmingly represented, although it is difficult to say whether their representation is disproportional. The largest Arab American demographic is composed of Lebanese Americans, who also happen to be the group best represented in Arab American letters. The early days of Arab American literature were dominated by Lebanese Christians, but in recent years more diverse national and religious groups have been increasingly represented. Although writers of North African backgrounds still compose only a small portion of published Arab American writers, their contribution has been substantial and portends a much more diverse thematic and structural future for Arab American literature. However, writers from Persian Gulf nations—Bahrain, United Arab Emirates, Kuwait, Qatar—are very few, most likely because there is not a substantial gulf population of landed citizens in the United States. Most immigrants to the United States from the Arab world in general become skilled laborers or business owners, which also effects the productivity of potential writers.

In the rest of this chapter, I focus on a cross-section of Arab American writers of North African background: Anouar Majid and Laila Lalami, from Morocco, both of whose work is rooted in a Moroccan landscape but differs in style and scope; and Samia Serageldin, from Egypt, whose novel *The Cairo House* offers an intimate portrayal of Egyptian life in the post–World War II twentieth century.

Si Yussef

Anouar Majid is a noted scholar of Islam, postcolonial theory, and literature. His first book, though, is a novel, *Si Yussef,* which was originally published in the early 1990s and reissued by Interlink in 2005. Although the novel takes place exclusively in Morocco and deals largely with Moroccan history and politics, it is written in English and employs themes that are relevant to readers of all backgrounds.

Si Yussef is mostly a novel of men, developing from the point of view of its male characters, who dominate the action. The exception to this male presence is the character of Lucia, Si Yussef's Spanish wife, who plays an important symbolic role in the story. The novel's structure renders the majority of the story a flashback, as the narrator, Lamin, recalls his conversations with Si Yussef, an almost mythical figure who exerts a strong influence on Lamin's worldview and takes up the burden of narration, through Lamin's memories, a few times throughout the novel. Because Lamin's voice sometimes gives way to Si Yussef's, *Si Yussef* kind of meanders into separate stories, though it is tied together by the consecutive interactions of Lamin, Si Yussef, and Isaac Benkalim, an important influence on a younger Si Yussef.

This structure is reminiscent of the Sudanese writer Tayeb Salih's *Season of Migration to the North*, a novel published in Arabic but translated into and widely read in English. In *Season of Migration to the North*, Salih offers a pastiche of Joseph Conrad's famous novel *Heart of Darkness*, about the talkative Marlow's journey into the heart of Africa. *The Heart of Darkness* frames its story through Marlow's spoken dialogue as he tells the story of encountering the mysterious and maniacal colonist Kurtz. Salih does not necessarily reproduce this structure, but at times he emulates it by having an unnamed narrator tell the story of the mysterious and brilliant Mustafa Saeed's journey to the heart of the global North, England. *Season of Migration to the North* is widely considered to be one of the most important twentieth-century African novels; part of its appeal lies in Salih's reworking of Conrad's themes and structure.

Si Yussef is a pastiche neither of *Heart of Darkness* nor of *Season of Migration to the North*, but its structure is reminiscent of both. Parts of it, such as the section "Beginnings," rely on a dialogue spoken by one character (Si Yussef) as remembered by another (Lamin). Beyond this structural similarity, there are some notable aesthetic techniques in all three novels. All three, for instance, are allegories: *Heart of Darkness* of the bankruptcy of colonization and the European's descent into madness; *Season of Migration to the North* of the ambiguities of decolonization; and *Si Yussef* of Morocco's cultures and histories. The transfer of dialogue from Isaac Benkalim to Si Yussef to Lamin highlights the emergence of Morocco as a modern nation-state in the wake of French colonization. Si Yussef's wife, Lucia, helps construct the allegory by symbolizing a European presence in Morocco that is both exotic and quietly powerful. Another notable aesthetic technique among the three novels is their use of mysterious remembered characters (Kurtz, Mustafa Saeed, Si Yussef) who are never fully defined but play a crucial role in the novels' structural and philosophical development.

I point to these things not to undertake a detailed comparison of *Si Yussef* to *Heart of Darkness* and *Season of Migration to the North,* but to situate it in a particular context that involves allegory and dialogue in order to explore historical and political themes. *Si Yussef* is trained primarily on Morocco, in particular Morocco's emergence as an independent nation-state in the wake of France's colonial and administrative rule. It does not focus solely on Morocco, however; at times, it looks at Morocco's interaction with Spain, its nearby European neighbor, and with western Europe more broadly. The interaction with Spain is of note because of certain historical conditions, primarily the migration of Moroccans and other Africans into Spain, and because of its symbolic richness: the ten-mile-long Strait of Gibraltar, which separates Europe from Africa, signifies a sea change of culture and economics in a remarkably short physical distance. Morocco is the port of departure for nearly all African immigrants who hope to enter into Europe, and Spain is the port of arrival. This sort of movement has an enormous though markedly different historical precedent: the Moorish occupation of Spain during the Middle Ages, which helped create an Andalusian culture that is still celebrated in both Europe and Africa.

The interconnectivity of Spain and Morocco, then, is longstanding, a relationship exemplified in *Si Yussef* by the marriage of Si Yussef and Lucia, the Spaniard with whom the Moroccans are intrigued because of her beauty and her (probable) refusal to convert to Islam. At one point, Si Yussef proclaims, "I divorced history to stay with my wife," a grand pronouncement that emphasizes his attachment to her in addition to the cultural, religious, and geographical differences they have overcome.[1] Lamin, the narrator, later reveals the larger meaning of Si Yussef's proclamation: "I saw Spain, the seductress, whispering a future I hadn't imagined yet." He continues, "Not far from [the sprawling Moroccan neighborhoods], smoke rose from long, metallically built factories and curled on the blue horizon to confirm our irretrievable destiny: that we were determined to join the holy ranks of the blessed France, Spain, England, and who knows, maybe even America. After this, there was only land, cultivated by reluctant hands sensing wrenching uprootedness. Tangier was left behind; it was no more" (144). The passage is replete with symbolic meaning, starting with Lamin's pronoun usage: he employs "we" to refer to a national community, that of Morocco. But Morocco is situated within an Africa and a global South that is being subsumed into Europe. This phenomenon is powerful, possibly even unstoppable, as evidenced by the strong language Lamin uses to describe it; "irretrievable destiny" seems to be a redundancy that only affirms the inevitability of Morocco's uprootedness. This language also implies that forces larger than the individual and the nation are setting these phenomena into motion. It is a language buttressed by messianic words such as *holy* and *blessed,* which allude to the West's self-perception as well as to its exalted economic position. Lamin notes the emergence of the United States as a destination among Africans who have traditionally migrated to Europe.

Ashab's café is an important setting within this international dynamic. Si Yussef had become a regular at Ashab's café in his adulthood more than twenty years earlier, "disillusioned by the unenlightened attitude of his previous café's regulars towards his wife" (16). Ashab's café thus represents a progressive Morocco, but one that does not simply reinforce the conditions for emigration. It is a native space without being simplistic. The transactions of culture, history, and politics that compose Morocco are rehashed daily at Ashab's. It is where "the story of Si Yussef was told in a thousand tongues" (71). These tongues do not merely represent languages, but worldviews and histories. Morocco is too complex to define, too clear-cut to romanticize. Majid describes it in allegory, then, using Isaac Benkalim, Si Yussef, and Lamin to narrate into existence a nation that would otherwise disappear.

Secret Son

Laila Lalami's debut novel *Secret Son* resembles *Si Yussef* in important ways but diverges considerably from it stylistically and structurally. The two novels thematically explore the complex politics and history of Morocco along with a variety of North African and Islamic politics. Lalami uses allegory less directly, though, and underscores history and politics through various character conflicts both explicit and subtle. Although some of the characters and situations overlap, the novel presents a series of discrete plots and events. *Secret Son* might be classified as a bildungsroman, a "novel of education" or coming-of-age narrative focused mainly on a single protagonist. In the case of *Secret Son,* that protagonist is Youssef El Mekki, a young man from a Casablanca slum who undertakes an interesting journey from poverty to wealth and back to poverty again, with tragic consequences.

Despite the discrete plot elements in *Secret Son,* the novel contains some common themes, which I examine here: class, gender, religion, and social issues such as migration/immigration and cultural conflict. I also look at the aesthetic dimension of *Secret Son.* Although the novel appears to offer a typical linear narrative, its aesthetics have been an important addition to the Arab American literary corpus. The most conspicuous element of the novel is Lalami's conflation of political Islam with internal and external corruption. The external corruption is largely governmental, but it includes economic systems, imperial politics, and rampant nepotism. Whereas in *The Girl in the Tangerine Scarf* Mohja Kahf examines a range of spiritual and doctrinal aspects of Islam, *Secret Son* focuses largely on the use of Islam as an authoritative discourse by both governments and antigovernment opposition groups. Lalami invokes similar themes in her short story collection *Hope and Other Dangerous Pursuits.*

Secret Son is a character study of Youssef, who exemplifies many of the burdens of Morocco's society and politics as well as, more broadly, those of the Arab and Muslim worlds. Youssef resides in a Casablanca slum, Hay an Najat, with his mother, Rachida, a hardworking orphan who says little about her past. Youssef believes his father was Nabil El Mekki, a schoolteacher who died in a tragic accident. He learns, however, that Rachida's story is a lie when he sees a picture of a well-known businessman, Nabil Amrani, on the cover of *Casablanca Magazine* and realizes that the businessman is his father. It is Nabil's distinct features, in particular his blue eyes, that catch Youssef's attention. Youssef finally works his way into his father's life and assumes the existence of a privileged son of Morocco's upper class. Nabil's family does not accept Youssef, however, and Nabil ultimately rejects him. Youssef, hurt and humiliated, gravitates to an Islamist group, the Party, headquartered in Hay an Najat. The Party's leader, Si Hatim, convinces him to participate in the murder of a well-known journalist, Farid Benaboud, who has written critically of the Party, accusing it of corruption. Although it appears at first that Youssef will go through with the act, he changes his mind but is set up as the culprit by the government, which orchestrates a behind-the-scenes plan that allows it to be rid of the pesky Benaboud while appearing to be tough on terrorism.

Youssef's story is constantly tragic, then. His adventures in various sectors of Moroccan society render him an embodiment of the nation itself in that his choices and circumstances illuminate both its promise and its problems. Lalami packs numerous themes into the novel: political Islam; economic colonization; the roles and representations of Moroccan women; government corruption; class and social mores; skin tone/physiognomy as a marker of class mobility; and the power of biological lineage.

A major element of *Secret Son* is the idea that nothing can prevent a human from becoming corruptible given the right circumstances. Lalami's criticism of Morocco is systemic, focused on the inherent structures that impel people to respond to the demands for success that are imposed on the ambitious by a corrupt system. The complicated character transformations that Lalami presents point to antigovernmental sentiment leading to religious politics. But Lalami does not allow the religious politics to be viewed as uncorrupt. She therefore illustrates how social corruption actually conflates antigovernment sentiment and religious activism. All these issues converge in the character of Youssef, who embodies many of the novel's allegorical features.

The first allegory Lalami presents is that of social transformation in Morocco. The Party occupies a building that once housed the venerable Star Cinema, where Youssef used to see a variety of films, both Eastern and Western. Now the building is home to a highly energetic and zealous religious group, a comment on the structural and cultural changes in modern Moroccan society. It is not an accident that the Party chooses to roost in Hay an Najat. Its leaders depend for effective recruitment on the bounty of unemployed and frustrated young males that inhabit the neighborhood. Youssef views the Party mainly with detachment or indifference, but the Party is rooted in Hay an Najat in such a way that its influence is inevitable.

Class stratification pervades the novel. When Youssef meets a pretty, upper-class woman named Alia in class at the state university, she invites him over to her house, which leaves him dumbfounded: "What about your parents? he wanted to ask. What would they say if you brought a man to the house? In his neighborhood, no father would allow it because, as the hadith went, whenever a man is alone with a woman, Satan joins them as the third."[2] Lalami often presents a formulation in which the upper class is more socially liberal than the working or under class. This disjuncture of social mores according to wealth and status speaks to numerous things, primary among them a sense of traditional national belonging (often based on a nostalgic view of the past) on the part of the impoverished and a Western yearning (often based on an inflated sense of self-importance) on the part of the rich. This disjunction provides Lalami with a plethora of rich textual material, which she uses to set up various social, ethical, and religious conflicts.

Morocco's class structure is indivisible from physical appearance. Youssef, for instance, has "sky blue" eyes that are "out of place in Hay an Najat. You would expect his eyes on a Fassi, a descendant of the Moors, one of those pedigreed men who had for generations controlled the destiny of the nation" (11–12). It turns out, of course, that Youssef too is descended from those who control the nation's destiny. His father, Nabil Amrani, believes that his class superiority arises from his genteel European lineage. When his daughter, Malika, begins dating an American whose mother is from Brazil, Nabil utters disapprovingly, "He is very dark" (164), a sentiment he is unable to overcome. This emphasis on skin tone as a marker of civility and intelligence is a holdover from the French colonization of North Africa but also arises from a deeply embedded social structure in which the privileges of light skin are used by those who have it to justify their privilege. Lalami examines what such attitudes mean for justice and coexistence in Morocco.

Nabil's sense of cultural superiority means little when he and his wife travel to Los Angeles to visit Malika. He explains to Malika why they arrived so late. During a three-hour wait in immigration, Nabil learns exactly how he fits into the Western world he claims to access: "It was bad enough that they fingerprinted me, like a common criminal, but then they took me to another room for a full search, and then after that, we still had to wait an hour and answer more questions" (181). Malika is already schooled on these matters. She notes that "her race had been the biggest signifier about her in America" (266). Through these scenes of anti-Arab and anti–Muslim discrimination in the United States, Lalami complicates the rigid formulas of Moroccan society by showing how notions of race and civility shift across hemispheres and national boundaries.

Compounding the complex problems of class and corruption in Morocco is the role the Moroccan government plays in the country's social prejudice and religious zealotry. Lalami indicates that the rise of political Islam cannot be separated from the Moroccan state's failure to provide its citizens with an accessible economy and a legitimate democracy. These failures are exposed and internalized by Farid Benaboud, the most admirable character in the novel. When the government is hassling him for his controversial reporting, he asks Nabil for support, which Nabil is reluctant to provide. Farid implores, "What we're trying to do now is different. We're trying to show that the elite of this country, our academics, our activists, our business leaders, support freedom of expression and that they stand with us" (149). Unfortunately, Morocco's elite either do not support the sort of free press Benaboud wants or are too cowardly to speak on its behalf. The various social dysfunctions in the novel overwhelm the values Benaboud upholds, for he is the ultimate victim of corruption and extremism. Lalami highlights discordant sociocultural issues through the confluence of politicians and religious dissidents who carry out their conflict in his presence and on his body.

In all of this action, Youssef becomes a tragic figure, carried along by forces much larger than he can comprehend. He takes the fall for other people's moral failures. Lalami seems to fancy him a new Jay Gatsby, the protagonist of F. Scott Fitzgerald's famous novel *The Great Gatsby*. Like *The Great Gatsby*, Lalami's novel focuses on the false promises of wealth as an antidote to personal struggle. Both heroes, Gatsby and Youssef, initially experience the life of wealth but then harsh downfalls shortly thereafter. Unlike Jay Gatsby, however, Youssef has to live with the consequences of the human corruption that has engulfed him.

The Cairo House

We move to the other side of Africa for our discussion of Samia Serageldin's *The Cairo House*, a novel that takes place in Egypt and the United States. The protagonist is Gihan Seif-el-Islam (Gigi), who hails from a once-powerful Egyptian Muslim family and in her adulthood resides in New England. Gigi's father, Shamel, is the youngest brother of the pasha, an aristocratic politician who wielded much power as head of the Wahd Party during the reign of King Faruk in the Ottoman period.

Because the novel is so oriented in specific Egyptian history, I must give a brief overview of who these figures are and how Serageldin approaches them. King Faruk was the half-Egyptian, half-Albanian dictator in Egypt during the 1940s and early 1950s. In 1952, a group of young revolutionaries calling themselves the Free Officers overthrew Faruk and installed a socialist government, promptly distressing the West by nationalizing Egypt's resources and physical sites such as the Suez Canal. Gamal Abdel-Nasser emerged as Egypt's president and quickly became an iconic figure in Arab politics. (He remains the most iconic Arab politician of the twentieth century.) Although Nasser is still beloved by many Arabs and was well liked during most of his tenure as president, dissenters have noted some of his foolish policy decisions and his harsh treatment of opposition parties, in particular Egypt's Muslim Brotherhood.

Nasser earned his popularity by appearing to stare down Israel, Britain, and France when the three countries invaded Egypt after Nasser kicked the British out of the Suez Canal, an important trade route to the Southern Hemisphere. (I say "appearing" because his bravado was possible only through the support of an irate Dwight Eisenhower, who ordered the invading militaries to retreat.) On the domestic front, he moved swiftly to break up the wealth of the old elite and to socialize various government programs. In *The Cairo House*, Serageldin illustrates how these moves affect Gigi's family when Nasser goes after the pasha and other entrenched elites, confiscating much of their property, occasionally interning them, and having them monitored by his intelligence service. These sorts of actions are typical in the aftermath of a coup d'état, when the new regime targets the gentry both out of a longstanding ill will and because of the gentry's disproportionate wealth and privilege.

Nasser's emergence came at the end of Ottoman rule, the Turkish empire that ruled over much of the Arab world until the early twentieth century. The Free Officers represented both a political and a symbolic break from the Turks' unpopular rule and the dictatorial politics inscribed therein. *Pasha* is an Ottoman title, so Gigi's uncle is situated on the wrong side of Nasser's ideology.

I explicate these events because *The Cairo House* is an historical novel that uses actual figures in Arab history and politics (King Faruk, Nasser, Prince Bandar, Mohamed Heikal). It is also an autobiographical novel: Serageldin is the niece of Pasha Serageldin, from whom the character of the pasha in *The Cairo House* is modeled. The novel's title is the name of an actual estate that remains in Serageldin's family. Her personal history informs not only the novel's content, but also its point of view. The events in *The Cairo House* are told from the perspective of the elite and the landowners, not from the perspective of the impoverished and the fellaheen (farmers, or those who tend the land). Readers should thus note that the novel's portrayal of Egypt and its modern politics is filtered through the author's particular experience. You can think of it as an historical novel with an autobiographical view of history.

Egypt's modern history frames Gigi's story, and upheaval in her life occurs simultaneously with moments of upheaval in Egypt. These upheavals are sometimes causally related, as when the famous writer Yussef El-Siba'yi is assassinated in Cyprus, a trip Gigi was supposed to have made, and Gigi realizes that "the bloody events [in Cyprus] had a domino effect on her life."[3] At one point, she reflects, *"That was the first time I became aware that my life was susceptible to being caught in the slipstream of history, that a speech broadcast over the radio could change my life forever. The year I first became aware of the burden of belonging: to a name, a past"* (20, italics in the original in all instances). Gigi is indivisible from the historical circumstances that affect her life. Through her alienation, exile, and subsequent return to Egypt, she becomes a microcosm of a certain type of modern Egyptian, one who speaks French fluently and has access to European and American educational institutions.

Gigi does not seem entirely self-aware of her role in history or of the role of history in her life, though. She frequently attributes much of her evolution to some undefined notion of destiny. In the novel's prologue, she asks herself a series of hypothetical questions, such as *"What if I had not run away to France?"* (4). Later, in another italicized section, she wonders, *"What if she had never met him again, that stranger from across the sea . . . ?"* (128). This form of speculation happens throughout the novel. It suggests that Gigi is not completely happy with the choices she has made or that she is thankful for not making choices about which she hypothesizes. Either way, she constantly assesses the past in order to make sense of current predicaments.

Serageldin creates a sense of Egyptian life through exploration of other issues. In addition to Nasser's rule, she looks at society under Nasser's successor, Anwar Sadat, the rise of Islamist politics, and matters of gender and class in Egypt. Her view of Sadat is more favorable than of Nasser, whom she criticizes heavily throughout the novel, but she seems displeased with any sort of politics not represented by the pasha's Wahd Party. She is also strident in her opposition to Islamist politics. Indeed, at one point she intimates a dislike of those who articulate religiosity through dress or appearance in general. When Gigi's aunt Zohra puts on *hijab* in her old age, Gigi thinks, "Yet here she was, if not veiled, at least with her head covered: she wore a white turban all the time now. If it were only women of her age, with eternity looming close at hand, it would be understandable. But I had seen women of all ages and backgrounds in Islamic dress all over Cairo" (157). At other points, Islamists are referred to as crazy and as terrorists. *The Cairo House* thus employs an ardently secular worldview, sometimes at the risk of totalizing religious Muslims or Egyptians who happen to dress conservatively as Islamists.

The novel's examination of class is of particular interest. I noted earlier that *The Cairo House* is told from the perspective of the wealthy pasha and his family; this perspective results in a view of Cairo's poor that reduces them to indistinguishable masses. Serageldin, in fact, often describes poor Egyptians as impulsive or mindless, or, at least, her language insinuates that they contain these qualities. When explaining what might happen if a pedestrian with a child is hit by a car on Cairo's streets, Gigi suggests, "The mild-mannered crowd around you will instantly turn into a mob, the mindless rage of the have-nots welling up from unsuspected depths of frustration and despair" (153).

Gigi previously observes of Cairo, "This is a society without safety-nets; the most expensive cars are prohibitive to insure and the run-of-the-mill, past-its-prime compact not worth insuring. It follows that the millionaire in his Mercedes is far more vulnerable than the poor drudge in his beat-up Fiat" (152). One might argue that the phrase "poor drudge" is patronizing or even disdainful, but it is more clear-cut that Serageldin presents a remarkably dim view of the situation given that the millionaire driver of the Mercedes can afford another car and that wrecking it probably will not directly affect his livelihood, a proposition that likely does not exist for the driver of the Fiat. These observations centered around class, usually offered through Gigi's narration or point of view, are given throughout *The Cairo House;* taken together, they illuminate a particular sort of class stratification that renders Egypt a country with two distinct societies.

Through the story of Gigi and her extended family, Serageldin sets out to create a strong sense of place in modern Egypt. The novel's historical dimension, then, is its most notable feature. The Cairo House is a constant within continual change. No matter where Gigi's life takes her—England, France, New Hampshire—the Cairo House anchors her to a specific place in the world. One of the crises of the story occurs when the pasha's family meets to determine whether they should sell the property, a transaction that would involve Gigi's unlikable father-in-law, Kamal Zeitouni. The family ultimately retains the property, and in so doing they retain a physical and spiritual connection to their past, their ancestors, and their homeland. They also retain a connection to their future in Egypt through a physical structure that is more than just a home.

Conclusion

Although the demographic of writers of North African background within Arab America is small compared to the demographic of Levantines (an old colonial term denoting Lebanese, Syrians, Palestinians, Jordanians), the Arab American arts are increasingly expanding in scope and content thanks to North Africans' contributions. It is difficult to say whether there is such a thing as a unified Arab American community or not. On the one hand, the community, of course, adheres to variegated politics and cultural traditions, so in this sense there is no unified Arab American community, nor would it be desirable to have one even if it were possible.

On the other hand, what I have in mind is something more abstract. Is there a unified Arab American community in the sense that the term *Arab American* adequately represents those who are affiliated with it either by choice or by association? This is an ongoing question among Arab American community members and scholars, and my humble contribution to the conversation would be to suggest that the term is adequate to those who feel comfortable enough with it to help complicate its meaning. I bring up the question because as Arab American literature slowly moves away from its Syro-Lebanese (and mostly Christian) origin, Arab America itself becomes richer but harder to delineate. This fact is no accident: it is the difficulty of delineation that creates the richness.

9

Potpourri

Alicia Erian, Randa Jarrar, Susan Abulhawa

THE TITLE TO THIS CHAPTER is not a cop-out, really, but it seems like one because in studying Alicia Erian, Randa Jarrar, and Susan Abulhawa I tried and tried but could not find a common theme that might lend itself to a chapter title. Potpourri is not merely a default choice, but an accurate descriptor of the three writers vis-à-vis one another and the range of themes they cover. Each author comes from a distinct background and covers an original set of themes, though there is overlap among their work. Rather than pressing to highlight the overlap that does exist, I focus on some of the poetics and politics that make each of their novels unique.

The three novels are also a potpourri because each adheres to (or promotes) a version of history and a social worldview that barely resemble those of the other two authors. They therefore provide readers a solid sense of the stylistic and thematic heterogeneity that exists in modern Arab American fiction. As you might have noticed by this point in the book, the majority of Arab American fiction writers are women (the same is true, by the way, of Arab American playwrights, poets, and critics). It is only appropriate, then, that I end this book by examining the distinct voices of three Arab American women novelists.

Towelhead

Alicia Erian's first novel—she has also published a short story collection, *The Brutal Language of Love*—has been one of the most commercially successful Arab American books. Its critical reception has been mixed, however. In 2008, Alan Ball of *American Beauty* and *Six Feet Under* fame directed the movie version of *Towelhead,* which, like the book, received mixed reviews. One reason for this mixed critical reception is the overt sexual descriptions and heavy-handed ethnic imagery that the half-Egyptian Erian uses. Anything so explicit is bound to be controversial; one need not go further than the title to know that *Towelhead* is not shy of being explicit.

Before I move into a textual analysis, I would like to look briefly at some of the controversy that *Towelhead* has generated. I do so not to reduce the novel to sociologica, but to highlight how issues of ethnicity and representation are integral to Arab American literature, even if Arab American authors want nothing to do with those issues. (Alas, nobody is so lucky.) I should probably point out for the sake of transparency that I have criticized *Towelhead* and find parts of the novel to be objectionable. In particular, I find its use of the epithet *towelhead* problematic. It is not the use of an epithet per se that is distasteful; all kinds of epithets have been used in all kinds of literature to great effect. And any book that uses an epithet so prominently will be controversial, no matter how that epithet is used.

My problem with its use in *Towelhead* is not philosophical or political; it is aesthetic. As Erian uses it, the term does not advance any real understanding of prejudice against Arabs, Arab American culture, or the use of language to marginalize certain people. The term instead acts as a marketing device; the story Erian tells in *Towelhead* would have been nearly identical even without the presence of the term. In short, I believe that the word deserves a treatment far richer and more sophisticated than the one Erian provides. It exists in the novel mainly for shock value.

Of course, many people disagree with my reading. Literature is a fluid phenomenon that naturally lends itself to variegated interpretation, a fact that makes literature fun in addition to being intellectually and emotionally rewarding. So please feel free to disagree with my admittedly grumpy reaction to the novel's title. If for no other reason, the word *towelhead* is there to generate discussion. Revealing my feelings about it is intended to do the same.

In many ways, *Towelhead* is not about Arabs or the Arab American community; it focuses on a character, Jasira Maroun (named after Yasser Arafat), who happens to be of Lebanese origin on her paternal side. This ethnic background plays a role in Jasira's story, but it does not define or consume her. Sexuality is a more crucial theme in *Towelhead*. The thirteen-year-old Jasira has been living in New York with her mother, Gail Monahan, when Gail discovers that her live-in boyfriend, Barry, has developed a fondness for shaving Jasira's pubic hair. Jasira is promptly shipped to Houston to live with her father, Rifat, an event that is told succinctly at the novel's start: "My mother's boyfriend got a crush on me, so she sent me to live with Daddy. I didn't want to live with Daddy. He had a weird accent and came from Lebanon." Jasira's memories of Rifat are fuzzy, but she remembers that she does not like him: "Once I spilled some juice on one of his foreign rugs, and he told me that I would never find a husband."[1]

Jasira's memories turn out to be accurate. Rifat refuses to hug her when he meets her at the airport—"This is how we do it in my country," he explains brusquely—and wastes no time commencing his physical abuse: "In the morning, my father stood in the doorway and whistled like a bird so I would wake up. I went to the breakfast table in my T-shirt and underwear, and he slapped me and told me to go put on proper clothes" (3). In addition to being abusive, Rifat is distant and inattentive. His job with NASA has led him to the nondescript suburb in which he lives and to a professional life that consumes most of his time and energy. He is also an ardent supporter of the 1991 Gulf War, the period in which *Towelhead* takes place. But Rifat is not all bad; he has moments of understanding, and he can actually be humorous. On a few occasions, he seems to want to do the right thing by Jasira, even if he does not know how. Overall, though, he is a brutish and unlikable character. Erian ties his brutishness and unpleasantness directly to his Lebanese ethnicity.

Many of the characters, in fact, conform to some type of entrenched social truism: Rifat, the innately violent and irrational Arab male; Mr. Vuoso (Travis), the aggressive white military brute; his ten-year-old son, Zack, the out-of-control white brat; Thomas Bradley, the oversexed black teenager; Gil and Melina Hines, the liberal do-gooders. Most important of all, we have Jasira, the confused teenager who accepts the sexual advances of older men. Jasira's sexuality is the most crucial (and shocking) aspect of *Towelhead*. It might be unfair to suggest that she welcomes Mr. Vuoso's behavior, but she is certainly intrigued by it, in no small part because of her own father's distance. Mr. Vuoso's sexual innuendos and body language finally give way to physical engagement, culminating in a bizarre, erotic sexual assault. This is the point at which Erian stretches her characters to the logical conclusion they will inevitably reach if they are not reigned in: the confused, flirtatious teenager is assaulted by the forceful, jingoistic bully. The good white liberals, of course, step in to protect Jasira from both Mr. Vuoso and her irrationally violent Arab father. There is, however, one thing on which Mr. Vuoso and Rifat can agree: Jasira should not hang out with Thomas, the oversexed black teenager. Nobody seems to like Zack.

Towelhead trades in this sort of shocking presentation. Jasira is coming into a familiarity with her sexuality at the same time as she is exploited in various ways by the adults in her life. She becomes aware that her sexual desirability allows her a sort of power over those who would ignore or mistreat her. Jasira never harnesses her sexuality, though, and moves without guidance into precarious situations. Rifat's irascibility only makes her evolution into sexual adulthood more difficult, as she has to sneak around to find tampons, which Rifat does not allow, and to deal with her burgeoning maturity without useful adult guidance. Jasira is thus a victim of her own biological transformation as well as a victim of irresponsible adults.

Erian rarely portrays Jasira's sexuality as beautiful. She generally shows it instead to be an inducement to illicit pleasure. Jasira's body is the site of a multifaceted struggle, one that pits characters' sensibilities and beliefs in a single site of contestation: Mr. Vuoso's racist patriotism, Rifat's strictness, Barry's perversity, even Gil and Melina's liberal altruism. Jasira herself participates in this contestation by simultaneously harnessing and performing her sexuality. Many of the contests played out on Jasira's body, like many sexual acts in general, have to do with control, wherein her body assumes a metonymical role. (Metonymy is a trope in which one thing is used to stand in for something else with which it is associated; in the case of *Towelhead*, Jasira's body is metonymical of each character's desires and impulses.)

This fact becomes clear in an exchange between Gail and Rifat:

> "She does what she wants," Daddy said. "I can't control her."
> "What do you mean you can't control her? That's why I sent her down here."
> "I can't control her," Daddy repeated. "Period. That's it. She's uncontrollable."
> "You're a grown man!" my mother said.
> My father didn't say anything. He just shrugged. (147)

Rifat's acknowledgment that, despite his manhood, he cannot control Jasira is out of character for him, so the reader suspects that he is feigning weakness in order to upset his ex-wife. However, it is as likely that Rifat has become aware of Jasira's involvement with other men. His inability to control these relationships further demasculinizes him, causing him to resent Jasira when he is not withdrawn from her.

If rebelling can act as a form of control for Jasira (as it often does or tries to do for teenagers), then the DNA she inherited from Rifat presents her with what seems to be two insurmountable challenges: her ethnicity, as exposed by her physiognomy, and the entrenched racism in the United States. She quickly learns where she exists in the social hierarchy of her new school in Houston. "By the end of class," she reflects, "everyone was calling me a towelhead. They also called me a sand nigger and a camel jockey, which I'd never heard of before. Even Thomas Bradley, who was black, called me a sand nigger" (54). Erian's use of these epithets is noteworthy for a couple of reasons, one in relation to race matters in the United States and the other in relation to the importance of geopolitics on domestic culture.

In terms of race matters, Jasira's identification of Thomas's ethnicity reveals her tacit understanding of American racial hierarchies. On one level, she finds it surprising that somebody who has experienced racism as an African American would participate in acts of racism against somebody else, especially when it employs a derogatory term historically used against African Americans. Thomas, who later apologizes to Jasira and ends up engaging her in multiple sexual acts, is likely responding to his powerlessness by welcoming Jasira into a place on the racial hierarchy that for once is lower than his. On another level, all of Jasira's tormentors are responding to the onset of the Gulf War, which was widely covered in 1991. (It is often called the first multimedia war because cable news networks, then still relatively new, covered it around the clock with never-before-seen technology.) Erian identifies a connection between US foreign policy and the treatment of ethnic communities inside the United States. In particular, she points to a common phenomenon in American history: members of the same ethnic group with whom the United States is engaged militarily overseas become subject to increased scrutiny and unfortunately an amplified racism. Jasira is a victim of a unique American tradition.

In conjunction with these specific phenomena, *Towelhead* comments on the dysfunction that lies beneath the seemingly idyllic life of the suburbs. The most obvious type of dysfunction exists in the sexual deviance exemplified by Mr. Vuoso. He subtly encourages Jasira's sexual curiosity, but that is not what accounts for his deviance. It arises from his need for power, which, like many

American males (and men everywhere), he conflates with sexual prowess. His anti-Arab racism does not deter him from seeking Jasira, but rather it makes her more desirable because an important dimension of that sexual prowess is a desire or a need to control her, something nobody seems able to do. By controlling her sexually, Mr. Vuoso can finally make her culture palatable and comprehensible.

Towelhead is not always so depressing, though. Its subject matter is deadly serious, but it is actually something of a light read with a straightforward narrative and a cheerful tone. Jasira's narration is generally matter-of-fact, sprinkled with some irony and some humor, both explicit and understated. And Erian appears to be aware that the characters read like clichés, for many of them act a bit too self-consciously to be completely sincere. Rifat, for instance, is so brusque at times he becomes oddly endearing. These complex personalities, *Towelhead* illustrates, merely represent the everyday contradictions in the underbelly of suburbia.

A Map of Home

Randa Jarrar's first novel resembles in parts some of its Arab American predecessors, but in total it is unique. Jarrar has said that she wanted to write the Arab American novel that she always would have liked to read, which probably accounts for its uniqueness; she obviously never would have written *A Map of Home* had such a book already existed.

Jarrar luckily found a gap in the Arab American literary tradition and filled it. The novel with which she filled it is indeed unlike anything that has been published before it by Arab American writers. *A Map of Home* is by turns and sometimes all at once funny, moving, lewd, introspective, crass, sarcastic, witty, crude, and sincere. It does not necessarily have one unified theme. If it is about anything in particular, it would be the eclectic life of its protagonist and narrator, Nidali Ammar. Nidali is thoroughly unconventional, beginning with her name: *nidal* means "struggle," and it has been used regularly in some form by members of the Palestinian resistance; adding the *i* to it renders it possessive, meaning "my struggle." It is a name that Nidali's mother, Fairuza (Ruz), is not exactly happy about. Moments after Nidali is born, she screams to her husband, Waheed, "I'm changing the girl's name right this instant! First you give her a stock boy's name, as though she'll be raised in a refugee camp, as though she's ready to be a struggler or a diaper-warrior, then you add a letter and think it's goddamn unique."[2]

Ruz, who wants to name the child "Sonatina," somehow never manages to get the name changed.

The scene of Nidali's birth sets the novel's tone, including as it does a vicious yet humorous fight between her parents, replete with colorful language, and a narrative that oscillates between serious and lighthearted. The colorful language persists throughout the novel, achieving at times a poetic status. Not only are Jarrar's characters unafraid to cuss, but they are quite adept at it. This cussing illuminates their ability to use language creatively and to articulate a range of emotions through spoken discourse. From a structural standpoint, the cussing is ironic: rather than adding gravity to the novel, it actually lightens the book by rendering difficult situations easier to handle. Jarrar does an excellent job of translating into English the flair Arabs have for innovative cursing.

The following exchange makes a good example:

> "I wanted to give you these," she said, and handed me a heart-shaped box.
>
> "What the fuck is that?" I said, shocked at the box.
>
> She slapped my mouth gently, "Why 'fuck'? Always 'fuck.' Fuck this, fuck them, fuck her, fucking A, fuck that, fucking stupid, fuck me, fuck you."
>
> "Whoa," I said, "that was cool. Can you say it again?"
>
> "Fuck you," she said. (288)

The dialogue here does not merely exhibit a humorous verbal flair. As in other parts of the novel, Jarrar combines a touching moment with a comical presentation, making the exchange ironic.

For instance, although there is a cheeky element to the naming of Nidali, there is something touching about it, too. Like Jarrar, Nidali is of Greek and Egyptian background maternally and of Palestinian background paternally. This Palestinian background is crucial to Nidali's identity. As she explains, "Baba said that moving was part of being Palestinian. 'Our people carry the homeland in their souls,' he would tell me at night as he tucked me in" (9). Nidali fulfills this identity, moving from Boston to Kuwait to Egypt to Austin, Texas. Along the way, she experiences a plethora of moral and social adventures that generate an eventful coming-of-age story.

A Map of Home does not much resemble *Towelhead*, but they have one theme in common: both are told from the point of view of teenage girls (though Jarrar includes Nidali's preteen years), and both explore their protagonists' burgeoning sexuality. Jarrar's exploration of Nidali's sexuality is as explicit as Erian's treatment of Jasira's, but Jarrar's style and focus are substantially different. Jarrar, first of all, explores healthier teenage relationships in which genuine affection exists. She also highlights Nidali's affection for masturbation. Most important, though, she includes lesbianism in her portrayal of Nidali's sexuality and is thus one of the first Arab American novelists to treat this theme seriously. A young Nidali who has moments of sexual tension with a female friend eventually becomes a Nidali who readily enters into a bisexual identity. This identity, along with her mixed background, makes her unorthodox in every possible way. Not only does she have a free spirit, but she also fails to conform to any of the typical characteristics inscribed in the categories of sexuality, religion, culture, and gender. She not only crosses boundaries; she conflates them as well.

An interesting facet of Nidali's life is that her father lives vicariously through her despite the fact that he has a son, Gamal. When Nidali wins a Quranic recital contest, an intricate art, she observes, "I was happy I'd won . . . or at least come in as one of three finalists. But something told me Baba was happier. This truth upset me. His happiness didn't seem to stem from a place of pride, but rather from the source where feelings of accomplishment reside. It was almost as though *he'd* won" (57). When Nidali later asks her father if she can become a singer, he replies, "Never. Singing is not bad, but you can do better. You can be a doctor! A big professor of literature! Write poetry like I used to do" (65).

These comments underline Waheed's complexity. Motivated by an active temper, he sometimes does terrible things, regularly beating his wife and children. He foists his expectations onto Nidali and does not allow her the sort of freedom she covets. Yet at the same time he is sometimes likeable, sympathetic even. He is passionately anticolonial and believes profoundly in the repatriation of Palestinians. He is also more a dreamer than a cynic. Take his response to Nidali's query about singing. His tendency to live vicariously through Nidali is evident, but so is a sincere concern that Nidali, whom he clearly admires, fulfill what he believes to be her special potential. Waheed is not the stereotypical Arab male of American lore, though he does exhibit a need for too much control over Nidali's decisions. Nevertheless, he is too multifaceted to be read as a simple representation of one or a few things: he fits nicely into Jarrar's pattern of writing contradictions into singular characters and situations.

Nidali feels Waheed's pressure and fluctuates between outright resentment toward him and moments of genuine affection. A really interesting exchange occurs between the two when Nidali flinches, expecting her father to hit her:

> Baba turned to me. "Have you been smoking hashish in the stairwell?"
>
> "Baba, I thought you were going to hit me."
>
> "Why would I do that?"
>
> "Because you hit me a lot."
>
> "No, I don't."
>
> "Yes, you do."
>
> "I don't hit you that often."
>
> "Ha!"
>
> "I've hit you five times in my life."
>
> I couldn't believe Baba was this deeply in denial. (132)

Waheed is definitely in denial. After all, as Nidali recounts, "Gamal and I compared our bruises like bomb sites on two different maps" (176). His denial does not bespeak ignorance or idiocy; it bespeaks a real shock that he behaves in a way that so starkly contravenes his self-image. There is a disjunction within Waheed's consciousness that makes this sort of denial, however unlikely, possible. He does not like to think that he beats his daughter, but he cannot seem to function on a day-to-day level without beating her.

Another moment that reveals Waheed's tenderness occurs when Nidali sketches an outline of Palestine and then asks him whether she did it correctly. Waheed cannot say whether her sketch is correct or not, eventually explaining, "There's no telling where home starts and where it ends," before he walks away in tears (193). His personal complexity reflects the complexity of his national identity as Palestinian, an identity that can be loving, ambiguous, gratifying, and violent all at once. His suggestion that maps are dynamic and constantly changing carries with it an important political point that Jarrar introduces without resorting to didacticism (that is, preachiness or crass politicizing).

Maps seem fixed and neutral, but as Jarrar is aware, they are highly political. Depicting Israel as Palestine, for example, will invoke Israelis' ire, whereas depicting the West Bank as Judea and Samaria (Jewish settlers' terms for it) will anger Palestinians. In this way and many others, maps can either subtly or explicitly betray the mapmaker's biases. As Waheed points out, "When it comes to maps, accuracy is always a question of where you stand" (189). For him, the map of Palestine is necessarily unstable because the borders of the nation that it once comprised are constantly changing owing to Israeli colonization. This instability is commensurate with the complicated lives of the Ammar family, whose members must constantly redraw maps to itinerant homes.

Nidali comes to understand better the instability of belonging and aspiration. Her map of home does not move in any single direction. She often describes things in cartographic terms: places in her high school in Austin, Kuwait's relationship to the United States, her sense of identity in a constantly evolving world. She is often inspired by her mother's wisdom about all things lasting and transitory. *A Map of Home*, in fact, is filled with characters worth closer attention than what I have been able to provide here. It is a novel that, like the promise of its title, does not lead readers toward a single place of resolution, but to a site of infinite possibility.

The Scar of David

Susan Abulhawa's novel *The Scar of David,* subsequently updated as *Mornings in Jenin,* does not much resemble *Towelhead* or *A Map of Home.* (If it did, I would have to rename this chapter, which would be a terrible inconvenience this far in.) The little it shares in common with *A Map of Home* has to do with Palestine and the dispersal of the Palestinian people. Abulhawa focuses almost exclusively on this subject, whereas Jarrar does so either peripherally or subtly. Of the novels I have examined in this book, *The Scar of David* most closely resembles Samia Serageldin's *The Cairo House.* Though each novel takes place in a different location and deals with a different set of circumstances, both are oriented around intergenerational historical events, and both are written with a comparable style that is sometimes proactive or didactic.

The Scar of David deals mainly with Palestinian dispossession, covering the period from 1941 to the 2002 Israeli massacre in the Jenin Refugee Camp. A very broad overview of this period in Palestinian history might be useful to readers of Abulhawa's novel, especially those readers who know little about modern Palestine. In 1880, on the eve of Zionism, a movement created by European Jews to settle another land and create a Jewish state, Palestine's population consisted largely of Arab Palestinians, around 75 percent Muslim with a 20 percent

Christian minority and smaller minorities of Jews, Druze, and Samaritans. Zionists gradually settled Jews into Palestine, culminating in a protracted conflict with Palestine's native inhabitants.

In 1948, when Israel was created, Zionist militias (primarily the liberal Haganah and the rightwing Irgun) displaced hundreds of thousands of Palestinians (estimates range from six to eight hundred thousand). The West Bank came under Jordanian rule and the Gaza Strip under Egyptian. In June 1967, amid increasingly audacious rhetoric from Egypt's Gamal Abdel-Nasser, Israel attacked Egypt, Syria, and Jordan and scored a quick, decisive victory in a conflict known as the "Six-Day War," the "1967 War," or the "June War." Israel occupied the West Bank and Gaza Strip, the Syrian Golan Heights, and Egypt's Sinai Peninsula, a space larger than Israel. Israel returned the Sinai to Egypt in the early 1980s as part of the famous Camp David Accords brokered by Jimmy Carter, but it later annexed the Golan Heights, which Syria still claims, and continues to occupy the West Bank and Gaza. Shortly after the 1967 War, Israel began settling Jews in the heavily populated West Bank and Gaza, in the process destroying Palestinian homes and farmland, leading to the tensions that have defined the Israel-Palestine conflict. Israel has since removed Jewish settlers from the Gaza Strip but continues to settle the West Bank with Jews, who have access to land, state infrastructure, and civil rights from which the West Bank Palestinians are excluded.

Other historical events Abulhawa highlights include Israel's 2002 invasion of Jenin, which set off an abundance of controversy in the United States, with Israel's supporters claiming that the Israel Defense Force killed only a few dozen militants, but the Palestinians pointing to a civilian massacre with death estimates ranging from sixty to more than one hundred; the first and second intifadas (the word *intifada* means a "shaking off" or "uprising"), which occurred in the late 1980s and early 2000s; the 1982 Israeli invasion of Lebanon, which entailed a heavy bombing campaign that led to much death and destruction and drove the Palestine Liberation Organization leadership to Tunisia; the Sabra and Shatila massacres, in which from fifteen hundred to three thousand Palestinian civilians were murdered by Lebanese Christian forces overseen by Israelis; and the 1983 bombing of the American embassy in Beirut.

Abulhawa's depictions of these events occur in the context of her characters' involvement in them. Members of the Abulheja family are either remarkably unlucky or textual emblems because all of the major twentieth-century incidents in the Middle East involve them or affect them adversely. If the conflict between Israel and the Arabs has been tragic, then the Abulheja family embodies the tragedy of conflict. Many of its members are killed or maimed by violence. Like many Palestinians, they are twice made refugees.

In terms of aesthetics, *The Scar of David* uses multiple points of view and does not follow a linear time sequence, bouncing from the present to the past, though much of the story is anchored around a conversation between siblings Amal Abulheja and David Avaram (née Ismael Abulheja) in Amal's house in Philadelphia. Abulhawa frequently employs the device of foreshadowing and sometimes resorts to a didactic tone, as when Amal observes that David "looked on in silence at the proof of what Israelis already know, that their history is contrived from the bones and traditions of Palestinians. The Europeans who came knew neither hummus nor falafel but later proclaimed them 'authentic Jewish cuisine.'"[3] This type of editorial comment appears consistently throughout the novel, lending it the feel of an essay at times. Because of its emphasis on actual events and its assertive political stances, the novel is a mixture of literary fiction and history lesson.

Its title accurately foregrounds its scope. At first, "the scar of David" may seem merely a pun denoting the injustice inherent in Israel's creation because the Israeli flag is adorned with a Star of David. Although this is one of the title's meanings, it has two additional, more substantive meanings: it describes one of David's physical features, a detectable scar on his face dating to his infancy; and it symbolizes an emotional scar that has plagued David throughout this life, resulting in an unshakeable liminality and alcoholism. David was not born as David; he was born as Ismael Abulheja, and although he is a Jewish Israeli, he is the brother of Amal, a Muslim Palestinian. David's adoptive father, Moshe, saw him as an infant and decided to steal him because his wife, a victim of repeated Nazi rape, was unable to conceive. Amid the hectic expulsion of Palestinians in 1948, Moshe snatched Ismael from his mother, Dalia, who spent the rest of her life wondering what happened to the child and feeling tortured over his loss. Ismael thus became David, though his telltale scar would finally reveal the secret his adoptive parents worked so hard to conceal.

The plot device of having a Palestinian child raised by Israelis is not exclusive to *The Scar of David*. Many Israeli and Palestinian writers have explored such possibilities—based on their imaginations or on actual events—as a way of high-lighting the interconnectedness of Jews and Palestinians or the ironies inherent in Israel's creation (e.g., Israel's being considered a model of liberation even while displacing others). The most famous example is the Palestinian writer Ghassan Kanafani's novella *Returning to Haifa,* a book that *The Scar of David* is reminiscent of philosophically and politically, if not structurally. In *Returning to Haifa,* Kanafani tells the story of a Palestinian infant left behind in an apartment when his parents flee amid the chaos of war. Twenty years later his parents return to the apartment in Haifa from the West Bank and find that their son has become an Israeli soldier and a devout Jew who wants little to do with them.

The main philosophical premise of this sort of story is simple but germane: culture is constructed through environment and experience, not inherited as a fixed characteristic. A biologically Arab child, therefore, can become Jewish if he is raised as a Jew, just as a biologically Chinese child can become an Arab if she is raised as one. (Comedian Dave Chappelle's famous "Black White Supremacist" skit is a humorous version of the same premise.) In *Returning to Haifa,* Dov (née Khaldoun) is uninterested in becoming "Arab" after meeting his biological parents; he tells them that he was always a Jew and will continue to be one. In *The Scar of David,* David/Ismael has a more complicated experience.

This complicated experience is attributable to numerous factors, primarily the painful fact that when David is a young soldier in the Israeli Defense Force during the 1967 War, he and fellow Israelis capture his brother, Yousef. David, although having some inkling that Yousef is not just another anonymous Palestinian, participates in ugly abuses against Yousef. David's military colleagues keep telling him that the Palestinian they have captured looks exactly like him, confirming his prior suspicions, a connection that Yousef makes with even more certainty: "'It was him!' Yousef said. 'I saw the scar! He's alive and he's a Yahoodi they call David!'" (94). Many years later David confesses to Amal that as a young man he did terrible things to Yousef.

David's psychologically tortured position (much easier to bear, of course, than Yousef's literally tortured one) exposes his liminality, which plays a central role among Abulhawa's motifs. Is he an Israeli or a Palestinian? A Jew or a Muslim? These questions are appropriately never tidily resolved. Although David never renounces his Jewish upbringing—he continues to express love and affection for his adoptive parents Jolanta and Moshe—he gradually becomes more comfortable with the reality of his bloodlines. Not only does he finally make an effort to meet his birth sister, Amal, but he desires to move closer to what it means to be a Muslim Palestinian. "Will you teach it to me? The Fatiha?" he asks at one point, referring to the Muslim profession of devotion (323).

David's liminality is symbolized by his alcoholism, a result of his competing identities and his role in perpetuating a conflict that makes those identities nearly impossible to unite. He will never fully be embraced by Palestinians, particularly because of the deeds he committed as a Jew. And he has already been marginalized by Jews who have learned of his secret and are unhappy with his "impure" lineage. He cannot wish away that lineage, a reality exemplified by the physical reminder of it that adorns his face. Because his face was injured while he was still Palestinian, David's scar ties him to his birth origin. He thus becomes an allegory of Palestine itself: something stolen and yearning for a comfortable return to normalcy. His liminality stands in for the Israel-Palestine conflict in total.

For many Palestinians and their supporters, the Israel-Palestine conflict is no more complex than a classic instance of a colonial settlers' movement to displace natives in order to make room for themselves. This description accurately boils down the conflict to its most basic essence. However, part of the reason that the conflict is conceptualized as impossibly complex and thus intractable is the fact that Israel was created directly after the Jews emerged from the horrors of the Nazi Holocaust. Abulhawa is passionately, even stridently devoted to the so-called Palestinian cause, rendering *The Scar of David* an example of what Cherokee scholar Jace Weaver calls "communitist literature."[4] *Communitism* is a portmanteau word (a combination of two words to form a new one—for example, *brunch*) combining *community* and *activism;* Weaver uses the term to identify Native American literature that contains an activist dimension focused on the well-being of the communities it represents.

Abulhawa's communitist focus on the Palestinians, though, does not ignore Jewish narratives. In particular, she focuses on the Nazi Holocaust and its perniciousness through the character of Jolanta:

> Having lost every member of her family in death camps, Jolanta sailed alone
> to Palestine at the end of World War II. She knew nothing of Palestine or Pal-
> estinians, following only the lure of Zionism and the lush promises of Milk
> and Honey. She wanted refuge. She wanted to escape the memories of sweaty

German men polluting her body, of hunger, and depravity. She wanted to
escape the howls of death in her dreams, the extinguished songs of her mother
and father, brothers and sisters, the unending screams of dying Jews. (39–40)

Jolanta does not conceptualize herself as a settler or a colonizer; she views herself instead as a refugee seeking asylum, which is one of the great promises of
Zionism despite the reality that it is in fact a colonial movement. Jolanta thus
embodies some of the difficult moral questions that have arisen from Zionism.
Abulhawa does not necessarily absolve Moshe and Jolanta of their actions, but
she seeks to explain them so that their actions, whatever readers make of them,
are seen as the acts of pained humans rather than of anonymous sociopaths. In
this way, the Palestinians can be adequately represented without being accused
of indifference to the fate of the Jews.

David's allegory is particularly meaningful here: the desperate Holocaust
refugees take what they feel they need despite the pain it will cause those who
are being stolen from. If David represents the loss of Palestine, then his brother,
Yousef, symbolizes its redemption. Yousef's life is filled with intense pain, including the murder of his wife and child. For a large portion of the novel, it appears
that Yousef, finally having given in to the despair of constant loss, committed
a terrorist act by driving a truck bomb into the American embassy in Beirut in
1983. It turns out, though, that he never went through with the act. Like the Palestinians, he rejects irrationality and turns away from despair.

Conclusion

Potpourri is an appropriate symbol to represent Arab American literature. If we
look at potpourri as a metaphor, then the image it conjures is simple but compre-
hensive: potpourri usually entails varied pieces of flora tossed into the same bowl,
resulting in a delightful sensual mixture. In short, it is a conjoining of discrete
items into one larger entity. The individuality is still evident and remains important, but the pleasure and utility of potpourri lie in its collectivity.

The category "Arab American literature" is the vehicle into which literary
potpourri is mixed. The pieces being added to the mixture are growing more
and more diverse, speckled with colors representing a vast geography. The bowl,
some may say, has already overflowed. Our critical apparatus must respond
accordingly.

Notes

▼

Suggestions for
Further Reading

▼

Bibliography

▼

Index

Notes

2. Uses of the Lebanese Civil War in Arab American Fiction: Etel Adnan, Rawi Hage, Patricia Sarrafian Ward

1. Gary Hentzi and Anne McClintock, "Overlapping Territories: The World, the Text, and the Critic," in *Power, Politics, and Culture: Interviews with Edward Said,* edited by Gauri Viswanathan (New York: Vintage, 2001), 56.

2. Etel Adnan, *Sitt Marie Rose,* translated by Georgina Kleege (Sausalito, CA: Post-Apollo Press, 1982), 1; subsequent citations to this work are given as parenthetical page references in the text.

3. Mahmood Mamdani, *Good Muslim, Bad Muslim* (New York: Pantheon, 2004), 4.

4. Rawi Hage, *De Niro's Game* (Hanover, NH: Steer Forth Press, 2006), 54; subsequent citations to this work are given as parenthetical page references in the text.

5. Robert Fisk, *Pity the Nation: The Abduction of Lebanon* (London: Oxford Univ. Press, 2001), 94.

6. Patricia Sarrafian Ward, *The Bullet Collection* (St. Paul, MN: Graywolf, 2003), 86; subsequent citations to this work are given as parenthetical page references in the text.

3. Exploring Islam(s) in America: Mohja Kahf

1. Mohja Kahf, *The Girl in the Tangerine Scarf* (New York: Carroll & Graf, 2006), 5; subsequent citations to this work are given as parenthetical page references in the text.

2. Ali Behdad, *A Forgetful Nation* (Durham, NC: Duke Univ. Press, 2005), 10.

3. Quoted in Peggy Trytko, "Caught in the Crossfire: Mohja Kahf," *IU South Bend Preface,* Feb. 7, 2007, available at http://iusbpreface.wordpress.com/2007/02/07/.

4. Sex, Violence, and Storytelling: Rabih Alameddine

1. Rabih Alameddine, *Koolaids: The Art of War* (New York: Picador, 1998), 18, italics in the original; subsequent citations to this work are given as parenthetical page references in the text.

2. Rabih Alameddine, *I, the Divine: A Novel in First Chapters* (New York: W. W. Norton, 2001), 229; subsequent citations to this work are given as parenthetical page references in the text.

3. Waïl S. Hassan, "Of Lions and Storytelling," *Al Jadid* (Winter–Spring 2004), 36.

4. Ibid.

5. Lorraine Adams, "Once upon Many Times," *New York Times,* May 18, 2008.

6. Rabih Alameddine, *The Hakawati* (New York: Alfred A. Knopf, 2008), 291; subsequent citations to this work are given as parenthetical page references in the text.

5. The Eternity of Immigration: Arab American Short Story Collections
(Joseph Geha, Frances Khirallah Noble, Evelyn Shakir, Susan Muaddi Darraj)

1. Joseph Geha, *Through and Through: Toledo Stories* (St. Paul, MN: Graywolf, 1990), 32; subsequent citations to this work are given as parenthetical page references in the text.

2. Frances Khirallah Noble, *The Situe Stories* (Syracuse, NY: Syracuse Univ. Press, 2000), 5; subsequent citations to this work are given as parenthetical page references in the text.

3. Evelyn Shakir, *Remember Me to Lebanon* (Syracuse, NY: Syracuse Univ. Press, 2007), 102; subsequent citations to this work are given as parenthetical page references in the text.

4. Susan Muaddi Darraj, *The Inheritance of Exile* (Notre Dame, IN: Univ. of Notre Dame Press, 2007), 112; subsequent citations to this work are given as parenthetical page references in the text.

5. Lisa Suhair Majaj, "New Directions: Arab-American Writing at Century's End," in *Post Gibran: Anthology of New Arab American Writing*, edited by Khaled Mattawa and Munir Akash (Bethesda, MD: Jusoor, 1999), 75.

6. Promised Lands and Unfulfilled Promises: Laila Halaby

1. Laila Halaby, *West of the Jordan* (Boston: Beacon, 2003), 206; subsequent citations to this work are given as parenthetical page references in the text.

2. Steven Salaita, interview with Laila Halaby, *RAWI Newsletter* (Summer 2008), 2.

3. Laila Halaby, *Once in a Promised Land* (Boston: Beacon, 2007), 31; subsequent citations to this work are given as parenthetical page references in the text.

4. Hayan Charara, "Introduction," in *Inclined to Speak: An Anthology of Contemporary Arab American Poetry*, edited by Hayan Charara (Little Rock: Univ. of Arkansas Press, 2008), xxvi.

7. Crescent Moons, Jazz Music, and Feral Ethnicity: Diana Abu-Jaber

1. Alice Evans, "Half and Half: A Profile of Diana Abu-Jaber," *Poets and Writers Magazine* 24 (1996), 42.

2. Email correspondence from Abu-Jaber to the author, October 2000.

3. Evans, "Half and Half," 43.

4. Diana Abu-Jaber, *Arabian Jazz* (New York: Harvest, 1993), 67; subsequent citations to this work are given as parenthetical page references in the text.

5. Qtd. in Evans, "Half and Half," 47–48.

6. Ibid., 41.

7. Carol Fadda-Conrey, "Arab American Literature in the Ethnic Borderland: Cultural Intersections in Diana Abu-Jaber's *Crescent*," *MELUS* 31, no. 4 (2006), 195.

8. Diana Abu-Jaber, *Crescent* (New York: W. W. Norton, 2003), 20; subsequent citations to this work are given as parenthetical page references in the text.

9. Diana Abu-Jaber, *Origin* (New York: W. W. Norton, 2007), 255; subsequent citations to this work are given as parenthetical page references in the text.

8. From the Maghreb to the American Mainstream: Writers of North African Origin (Anouar Majid, Laila Lalami, Samia Serageldin)

1. Anouar Majid, *Si Yussef* (Northampton, MA: Interlink, 2005), 21; subsequent citations to this work are given as parenthetical page references in the text.

2. Laila Lalami, *Secret Son* (Chapel Hill, NC: Algonquin, 2009), 63; subsequent citations to this work are given as parenthetical page references in the text.

3. Samia Serageldin, *The Cairo House* (Syracuse, NY: Syracuse Univ. Press, 2000), 124; subsequent citations to this work are given as parenthetical page references in the text.

9. Potpourri: Alicia Erian, Randa Jarrar, Susan Abulhawa

1. Alicia Erian, *Towelhead* (New York: Simon and Schuster, 2005), 1; subsequent citations to this work are given as parenthetical page references in the text.

2. Randa Jarrar, *A Map of Home* (New York: Other Press, 2008), 6; subsequent citations to this work are given as parenthetical page references in the text.

3. Susan Abulhawa, *The Scar of David* (Summerland, CA: Journey, 2006), 100; subsequent citations to this work are given as parenthetical page references in the text.

4. See Jace Weaver, *That the People Might Live: Native American Literatures and Native American Community* (Oxford, UK: Oxford Univ. Press, 1997).

Suggestions for Further Reading

Nonfiction

Elmaz Abinader: *Children of the Roojme* (1991)

Diana Abu-Jaber: *The Language of Baklava* (2005)

Etel Adnan: *In the Heart of the Heart of Another Country* (2005)

Leila Ahmed: *A Border Passage: From Cairo to America—A Woman's Journey* (2000)

Munir Akash and Khaled Mattawa, eds.: *Post-Gibran: Anthology of New Arab American Writing* (1999; mixed genre)

Barbara Nimri Aziz: *Swimming up the Tigris* (2007)

Jane Brox: *Five Thousand Days Like This One* (2000)

Suheir Hammad: *Drops of This Story* (1996)

Joanna Kadi, ed.: *Food for Our Grandmothers* (1994); *Thinking Class* (1996)

Pauline Kaldas: *Letters from Cairo* (2007)

Susan Muaddi Darraj, ed.: *Scheherazade's Legacy* (2004)

Naomi Shihab Nye: *Never in a Hurry* (1996)

Gregory Orfalea: *The Arab Americans: A History* (2005)

Edward Said: *Out of Place* (1999)

Steven Salaita: *Anti-Arab Racism in the USA: Where It Comes from and What It Means for Politics Today* (2006); *Arab American Literary Fictions, Culture, and Politics* (2006); *The Uncultured Wars: Arabs, Muslims, and the Poverty of Liberal Thought* (2008)

Evelyn Shakir: *Bint Arab* (1997)

Poetry

Elmaz Abinader: *In the Country of My Dreams* (1999)

Etel Adnan: *Moonshots* (1966); *The Arab Apocalypse* (1989)

Hayan Charara: *The Alchemist's Diary* (2001); *The Sadness of Others*

Marian Haddad: *Somewhere Between Mexico and a River Called Home* (2004)

Suheir Hammad: *Zaatardiva* (2006)

Nathalie Handal: *The Neverfield* (2005); *The Lives of Rain* (2005)

Samuel Hazo: *Just Once: New and Previous Poems* (2002); *Thank a Bored Angel* (1983)

Dima Hilal: *Ghaflah: The Sin of Forgetfulness* (2005; performance poetry on CD)

Lawrence Joseph: *Into It* (2005); *Codes, Precepts, Biases, and Taboos* (2005)

Mohja Kahf: *E-Mails from Scheherazade* (2003)

Khaled Mattawa: *Zodiac of Echoes* (2003); *Ismailia Eclipse* (1997)

D. H. Melhem: *New York Poems* (2005)

Eugene Paul Nassar: *Wind of the Land* (1979)

Naomi Shihab Nye: *You and Yours* (2005); *19 Varieties of Gazelle* (2002); *Words under the Words* (1994)

Gregory Orfalea: *Capital of Solitude* (1988)

Gregory Orfalea and Sharif Elmusa, eds.: *Grape Leaves: A Century of Arab American Poetry* (2000)

Ameen Rihani: *Hymns of the Valleys* (1955; posthumous)

David Williams: *Traveling Mercies* (1993); *Far Sides of the Only World* (2004)

Fiction

Kathryn K. Abdul-Baki: *Tower of Dreams* (1995); *Ghost Songs* (2000)

Diana Abu-Jaber: *Arabian Jazz* (1993); *Crescent* (2003); *Origin* (2007)

Susan Abulhawa: *The Scar of David* (2006)

Etel Adnan: *Sitt Marie Rose* (1978); *Of Cities and Women (Letters to Fawaz)* (1993)

Rabih Alameddine: *Koolaids: The Art of War* (1998); *I, the Divine: A Novel in First Chapters* (2002); *The Hakawati* (2008)

miriam cooke: *Hayati* (2000)

Alicia Erian: *Towelhead* (2005)

Joseph Geha: *Through and Through: Toledo Stories* (1990)

Kahlil Gibran: *Broken Wings* (1912)

Rawi Hage: *De Niro's Game* (2006)

Laila Halaby: *West of the Jordan* (2003); *Once in a Promised Land* (2007)

Samuel Hazo: *Stills* (1989)

Randa Jarrar: *A Map of Home* (2008)

Mohja Kahf: *The Girl in the Tangerine Scarf* (2006)

Pauline Kaldas and Khaled Mattawa, eds.: *Dinarzad's Children* (2004)

Laila Lalami: *Hope and Other Dangerous Pursuits* (2005); *Secret Son* (2009)

Angela Tehaan Leone: *Swimming toward the Light* (2007)

Anouar Majid: *Si Yussef* (2005)

Susan Muaddi Darraj: *The Inheritance of Exile* (2007)

Mikhail Naimy: *Memoirs of a Vagrant Soul* (1952)
Frances Khirallah Noble: *The Situe Stories* (2000)
Naomi Shihab Nye: *Habibi* (1999; teen fiction)
Ameen Rihani: *The Book of Khalid* (1911)
Samia Serageldin: *The Cairo House* (2000)
Evelyn Shakir: *Remember Me to Lebanon* (2007)
Patricia Sarrafian Ward: *The Bullet Collection* (2003)

Notable Anglophone Arab Novels

Leila Aboulela: *Minaret* (2005); *The Translator* (2006)
Fadia Faqir: *Pillars of Salt* (1998)
Hisham Matar: *In the Country of Men* (2006)
Ahdaf Soueif: *The Map of Love* (2000)

Bibliography

Abu-Jaber, Diana. *Arabian Jazz*. New York: Harvest, 1993.

——. *Crescent*. New York: W. W. Norton, 2003.

——. *Origin*. New York: W. W. Norton, 2007.

Abulhawa, Susan. *The Scar of David*. Summerland, CA: Journey , 2006.

Adams, Lorraine. "Once upon Many Times." *New York Times,* May 18, 2008.

Adnan, Etel. *Sitt Marie Rose*. Translated by Georgina Kleege. Sausalito, CA: Post-Apollo Press, 1982.

Alameddine, Rabih. *The Hakawati*. New York: Alfred A. Knopf, 2008.

——. *I, the Divine: A Novel in First Chapters*. New York: W. W. Norton, 2001.

——. *Koolaids: The Art of War*. New York: Picador, 1998.

Behdad, Ali. *A Forgetful Nation*. Durham, NC: Duke Univ. Press, 2005.

Charara, Hayan, ed. *Inclined to Speak: An Anthology of Contemporary Arab American Poetry*. Little Rock: Univ. of Arkansas Press, 2008.

——. "Introduction." In *Inclined to Speak: An Anthology of Contemporary Arab American Poetry,* edited by Hayan Charara, xiii–xxxiii. Little Rock: Univ. of Arkansas Press, 2008.

Erian, Alicia. *Towelhead*. New York: Simon and Schuster, 2005.

Evans, Alice. "Half and Half: A Profile of Diana Abu-Jaber." *Poets and Writers Magazine* 24 (1996): inclusive page nos. unavailable.

Fadda-Conrey, Carol. "Arab American Literature in the Ethnic Borderland: Cultural Intersections in Diana Abu-Jaber's *Crescent*." *MELUS* 31, no. 4 (2006): 187–205.

Fisk, Robert. *Pity the Nation: The Abduction of Lebanon*. Oxford, UK: Oxford Univ. Press, 2001.

Geha, Joseph. *Through and Through: Toledo Stories*. St. Paul, MN: Graywolf, 1990. Reprint. Syracuse, NY: Syracuse Univ. Press, 2009.

Hage, Rawi. *De Niro's Game*. Hanover, NH: Steer Forth Press, 2006.

Halaby, Laila. *Once in a Promised Land*. Boston: Beacon, 2007.

——. *West of the Jordan*. Boston: Beacon, 2003.

Hassan, Waïl S. "Of Lions and Storytelling." *Al Jadid* (Winter–Spring 2004): 36.

Hentzi, Gary, and Anne McClintock. "Overlapping Territories: The World, the Text, and the Critic." In *Power, Politics, and Culture: Interviews with Edward Said*, edited by Gauri Viswanathan, 53–68. New York: Vintage, 2001.

Jarrar, Randa. *A Map of Home*. New York: Other Press, 2008.

Kahf, Mohja. *The Girl in the Tangerine Scarf*. New York: Carroll & Graf, 2006.

Lalami, Laila. *Secret Son*. Chapel Hill, NC: Algonquin, 2009.

Majaj, Lisa Suhair. "New Directions: Arab American Writing at Century's End." In *Post Gibran: Anthology of New Arab American Writing*, edited by Khaled Mattawa and Munir Akash, 67–77. Bethesda, MD: Jusoor, 1999.

Majid, Anouar. *Si Yussef*. Northampton, MA: Interlink, 2005.

Mamdani, Mahmood. *Good Muslim, Bad Muslim*. New York: Pantheon, 2004.

Muaddi Darraj, Susan. *The Inheritance of Exile*. Notre Dame, IN: Univ. of Notre Dame Press, 2007.

Noble, Frances Khirallah. *The Situe Stories*. Syracuse, NY: Syracuse Univ. Press, 2000.

Salaita, Steven. Interview with Laila Halaby. *RAWI Newsletter* (Summer 2008): 4–5.

Serageldin, Samia. *The Cairo House*. Syracuse, NY: Syracuse Univ. Press, 2000.

Shakir, Evelyn. *Remember Me to Lebanon*. Syracuse, NY: Syracuse Univ. Press, 2007.

Trytko, Peggy. "Caught in the Crossfire: Mohja Kahf." *IU South Bend Preface*, Feb. 7, 2007. Available at http://iusbpreface.wordpress.com/2007/02/07/.

Viswanathan, Gauri, ed. *Power, Politics, and Culture: Interviews with Edward Said*. New York: Vintage, 2001.

Ward, Patricia Sarrafian. *The Bullet Collection*. St. Paul, MN: Graywolf, 2003.

Weaver, Jace. *That the People Might Live: Native American Literatures and Native American Community*. Oxford, UK: Oxford Univ. Press, 1997.

Index